D0552807

EMBRACING COMPASSION

Embracing Compassion

A Revolution in Leadership

Daisaku Ikeda

SELECTED ADDRESSES
VOLUME 1: 2001–2003

World Tribune
Press

Published by World Tribune Press
606 Wilshire Blvd.
Santa Monica, CA 90401

© 2009 Soka Gakkai

ISBN 978-1-932911-82-4

Cover and interior design by Gopa and Ted2, Inc.

All rights reserved
Printed in the United States of America

10 9 8 7 6 5 4 3 2

Contents

Editor's Note

"The mission of a leader is to put everyone's mind at ease," SGI President Daisaku Ikeda tells us on page 8 of *Embracing Compassion*, vol. 1. "Toward that end, it is very important to offer words and take actions that abound with compassion."

In August 2001, the first Soka Gakkai Nationwide Executive Conference met in Karuizawa. This conference has been held every summer since then. *Embracing Compassion*, volume 1, brings together President Ikeda's speeches at those gatherings from 2001 through 2003, while volume 2 comprises speeches from 2004 and 2005.

Although his words are directed to those who have taken responsibility in the Soka Gakkai International to care for each individual member, they offer significant lessons for us all.

The following abbreviations appear in some citations:

- GZ, page number(s)—refers to *Nichiren Daishonin gosho zenshu* (The Collected Writings of Nichiren Daishonin), the Japanese-language compilation of Nichiren Daishonin's writings (Tokyo: Soka Gakkai, 1952)
- LS(chapter number), page number(s)—refers to *The Lotus Sutra*, translated by Burton Watson (New York: Columbia University Press, 1993)

- OTT, page number(s)—refers to *The Record of the Orally Transmitted Teachings*, the compilation of Nichiren's oral teachings on the Lotus Sutra; translated by Burton Watson (Tokyo: Soka Gakkai, 2004)
- WND-1 and WND-2—refer to *The Writings of Nichiren Daishonin*, volumes 1 and 2 respectively (Tokyo: Soka Gakkai, 1999 [vol. 1] and 2006 [vol. 2])

Enact a Dramatic Life of Victory

Life is a drama. Since we are going to perform on the stage of life anyway, we ought to live vigorously and joyfully and enact an inspiring drama of successive victories. We have to win in life. We have to win in society. We have to win a resounding victory for *kosen-rufu*.

Toward that end, we need a supreme strategy that will ensure victory. What is required is iron unity—everyone uniting in spirit. We need to take courageous and meticulous action. We need the determination of an indomitable leader. In a sense, it was the great determination of Josei Toda, the second Soka Gakkai president, that resulted in the Soka Gakkai's present development. Also, by seizing the initiative we can gain the upper hand. In a struggle, it is necessary to be proactive. These are the secrets of an ever-victorious leader; these are the timeless and universal principles of victory.

President Toda used to say: "When we have won, we tend to sow the seeds of future defeat. Conversely, when we have lost, we can create the cause for future victory." He used to always admonish us, saying, "You must keep up your guard, even after a victory." When we are victorious—that is when we should rebuild the organization and solidify our footing.

Let us take the example of someone with a regional leadership position. The person may vaguely imagine that he or she is keeping watch over the entire region, but that's too general and abstract. We need to clarify the specific place and sphere of activities for which the person is responsible. We need to decide the person's home base. Then, on that foundation, he or she can carry out activities spanning the entire region.

To put on an air of self-importance and avoid having to do anything by keeping your responsibility vague while, at the same time, making others work hard, is sneaky and cunning. Leaders in the SGI must not have such an attitude. When leaders have such an arrogant attitude, everything comes crashing down.

Activities for *kosen-rufu* require enormous effort, but for that reason we can accumulate great benefit for ourselves in the present and also for our descendants well into the future. Therefore, to pass up the opportunity to take on this struggle would be our infinite loss.

Because there are enemies, we can exert ourselves. Because we energetically engage ourselves, we can accumulate benefit. And because we work hard, we can savor supreme joy.

From Division to Unity

The SGI movement is winning strong sympathy and support around the world. The other day, Dr. Winston Langley, acting provost and vice chancellor for Academic Affairs of the University of Massachusetts Boston, endorsed my 2001 SGI Day peace proposal in an interview with a correspondent of the *Seikyo Shimbun*, the Soka Gakkai's daily newspaper. *[On Jan. 26, 2001, President Ikeda presented his peace proposal "Creating and Sustaining a Century of Life: Challenges for a New Era," commemorating the twenty-sixth SGI Day. See the May 2001* Living Buddhism *for the full text.]*

A prominent political scientist, Dr. Langley is a person of profound erudition and rich character. He serves as an advisor to the Boston Research Center for the 21st Century, which I founded.

Dr. Langley observed that the world today is in many senses divided. He credited me with keeping my focus trained on global society amid all of this division and with bringing many disparate fragments together as part of a comprehensive outlook.

He also applauded my efforts to raise new questions and deepen the discussion about ways of thinking and events that people have come to take for granted. He suggested that I am advancing this work on the planes of philosophy, education and religion from the standpoint of universal humanism.

I have long affirmed that the twenty-first century will be a century of life. Needless to say, during the twentieth century, human life was treated with savage disregard. Now, at the start of the twenty-first century, human society is at last earnestly searching for a philosophy that upholds the sanctity of life. People are beginning to seek out a new humanism. In truth, the Age of Soka—an age in which the humanistic principles of Nichiren Buddhism gain wide acceptance—has arrived.

Our movement for *kosen-rufu* is a noble enterprise to put the Buddhist philosophy of the sanctity of life into practice in all areas of society. Let us take pride in advancing on the leading edge of the times.

Dr. Langley observed that the concept of symbiosis, which I discuss at length in the peace proposal, means creative coexistence in which each party seeks the good of all. Taking up the idea of humanitarian competition, which I introduce in my January 1996 peace proposal, he clarified that this does not mean competition in the usual sense but rather a situation in which all parties challenge themselves to achieve a common objective. It means shared struggle.

The educator noted that the English term *compete* originally referred to people coming together to face some challenge. When we base ourselves on this lofty perspective, he said, we can overcome negative competitiveness and work together to achieve our spiritual evolution.

Spread the Spirit of Japan's "Peace Constitution" Throughout the World

With regard to Japan's constitution, which is famous for its renunciation of war, Dr. Langley said that the essential question is not whether Japan ought to militarize but how the spirit of Japan's constitution can be spread to all people. In that regard, he affirmed, Japan can make a very important contribution to the world.

According to Dr. Langley, Japan's constitution can serve as a model not only for Japan but for all humankind and offers suggestions for the future scope of the United Nations. He also applauded my proposal that people should work in liaison with the United Nations toward lasting peace based on the principle and the spirit of Article 9 of Japan's constitution: "Aspiring sincerely to an international peace based on justice and order, the Japanese people forever renounce war as a sovereign right of the nation and the threat or use of force as means of settling international disputes. (2) In order to accomplish the aim of the preceding paragraph, land, sea, and air forces, as well as other war potential, will never be maintained. The right of belligerency of the state will not be recognized."

Dr. Langley's generous words are praise for all of you who are working to promote the spread of peace and humanism throughout the world. It is for this reason that I have taken the liberty of introducing Dr. Langley's comments. [*Dr. Langley also noted that while the development of modern thought has largely excluded life's spiritual side, people today are becoming aware of the need to revive spirituality and are genuinely seeking out spiritual leaders. In that context, he noted that President Ikeda's proposals, while based on Buddhism, do not seek to impose any particular religion on people. The educator added that he was grateful for the existence of a leader possessing such a grand and profound spiritual perspective.*]

Japan Invaded Asia in Imitation of the West

Professor Takehiko Furuta [formerly of Showa Pharmaceutical University], a leading authority on the ancient Japanese kingdom of Yamatai, sent me a copy of his paper in which he describes the essential nature of modern Japan's invasion of Asia: "It seems to me that Japan was trying to play catch-up with the imperialist West. It was a matter of imitation. Japan should realize the ugliness of its past actions and discard its posturing [in imitation of the West]."

He went on to say that even if the peoples of China, Korea and other countries in Asia did not seek an apology, Japan ought to apologize before all humankind. That would be the proper stance for the country to take, he said.

Professor Furuta stresses that the arrogance of Japanese militarism must not be revived. I agree entirely.

My four older brothers were drafted into the army. My eldest brother died in the war. Our home was burned down in the air raids. The root evil that caused the war was nationalism.

To ensure that this tragedy is never repeated, the people must become strong. That is the only way. The people must become wise. And the people must keep a strict watch over power. That is why the Soka Gakkai's advance is itself the advance of peace.

As it is still quite hot, please be sure to get adequate rest so that you can vigorously lead activities in good health.

From the August 9, 2001, Seikyo Shimbun

Make a New Departure!

AUGUST 7, 2001

Those who always resolve, "I will make a new departure!" and "I will construct something new!" will be victorious in the end. In contrast, those who think, "I've done enough already" are leading lives of defeat.

Buddhism is victory or defeat. Life is an eternal struggle. To the end, we should live with strength and vigor. In any realm of activity, reality is very strict. It is the power of Buddhism that enables us to win in any situation. Difficulties are inevitable in life—that is true for everyone. Herein lies a profound reason for our practice; we should always remember this.

The Soka Gakkai exists to widely propagate the Buddhism of Nichiren Daishonin. In the course of this struggle, there will naturally be times when we are faced with extreme hardship and difficulty. Nichiren Daishonin was fiercely attacked by people throughout Japan. Nevertheless, he dauntlessly took action to open a great and eternal path of hope for all humankind. We are carrying on the Daishonin's great legacy.

Nichiren said, "A person of wisdom is not one who practices Buddhism apart from worldly affairs but, rather, one who thoroughly understands the principles by which the world is governed"

(WND-1, 1121). Buddhism does not exist within a vainglorious monastery somewhere. It is neither abstract nor a fairy tale. It is found and its truth is borne out in society.

Nichiren Buddhism is focused squarely on human beings. Tsunesaburo Makiguchi and Josei Toda, the first and second Soka Gakkai presidents, steadfastly spread the teaching among the people, who were laboring under extreme suffering. Buddhism and the advancement of the Soka Gakkai exist in dedicating ourselves to others and imparting joy, causing flowers of happiness and victory to blossom, and in unfurling the banner of justice in society.

Advancing *kosen-rufu* comes down to propagating the teaching. Through such efforts, we are laying the foundation for an age of the people. Those who can actually expand *kosen-rufu* are genuine leaders. Those who cannot lack courage and are self-centered.

Put Everyone's Mind at Ease

The mission of a leader is to put everyone's mind at ease. Toward that end, it is very important to offer words and take actions that abound with compassion. This is in contrast to the authoritarian attitude of a person who tries to manipulate people as if they were machines, assuming that they will do whatever he says. The Soka Gakkai is a world of thoroughgoing humanism.

In all activities for *kosen-rufu*—such as the effort to expand subscriptions to our publications—we should always maintain a warm and humanistic spirit rather than try to whip up people's motivation with a lot of shouting. Unless we appeal to others with a genuine sense of camaraderie, with the spirit, "We're going to do this together," we cannot elicit any strong or warm resonance in people's hearts.

At any rate, as senior leaders, you should earnestly pray that everyone in your region enjoys good health and can joyfully accomplish his or her mission. And you yourselves should set an example for others through your actions. A leader who is indolent and who manifests the arrogance of authoritarianism is guilty of negligence.[1]

If a leader attends a meeting and gives guidance but no one at the meeting feels joy or is motivated to take action, then it is not genuine guidance. To make matters worse, if the central figure is curt and unsociable, that makes a mockery of everyone's efforts to gather in the first place.

It is important to sincerely and cheerfully thank people for their hard work and offer warm, heartfelt encouragement. I would like to ask that you use your ingenuity to affect a "meeting revolution" with the aim of making each activity interesting and significant for all participants.

False Rumors Can Undermine the Revolution

Today, to mark your new departure, I would like to present you with insightful words from around the world.

Soong Ching-ling, wife of modern China's great leader Sun Yat-sen, was hailed as the conscience of China. Madam Soong remarked, "We must keep close to our people."[2] The SGI likewise must always stand together with the people, advancing with the unity of "many in body, one in mind."

Madam Soong also said: "If we let false rumors and alarms disturb us, the revolution will be lost. But we shall stand firm, and the revolution will not be lost."[3] As leaders, we must not ignore malicious and groundless rumors. Without steadfastly refuting false allegations and those who propound them, we cannot protect the members.

Sun Yat-sen said, "To accomplish a great enterprise, above all one must possess great will, great daring, and great resolve."[4] The goal of *kosen-rufu,* toward which we are striving, is a most daring and ambitious undertaking. There is no higher ideal of justice. All of you are leaders of this vast and historic enterprise.

President Toda strictly admonished: "No matter how painful the situation, as a leader you should always be high-spirited and vigorous when you are in front of others. This will put your fellow members' minds at ease and win their support. Giving everyone hope and confidence is the role of a leader." I hope you will be model leaders who exemplify the principles of "faith manifesting itself in daily life" and "faith equaling excellent health." Each day, morning and evening, I strongly and deeply pray for your health and longevity.

The Buddhist Gods Protect Those With Pure Hearts

Next, I would like to introduce the words of the French literary giant Victor Hugo. In parliament, he issued this impassioned cry: "The people must not suffer! The people must not go hungry! That is the serious problem we face; that is the danger. That alone, gentlemen, and no other!"[5]

Hugo's sole concern was the happiness of the people. He also said, "To be a nation of ideals is to be a nation of justice; to be a people of beauty is to be a people of truth."[6] True beauty is to be found in the world of faith. Things like money or academic credentials have absolutely nothing to do with faith. People with beautiful hearts are most worthy of respect. Everyone admires such people, and all the Buddhas and Buddhist gods praise and protect them.

To Remain Silent Amounts to an Act of Betrayal

The German playwright Ernst Toller is well known as the first Jewish author to stand up to the Nazis. He wrote: "Beneath the yoke of barbarism one must not keep silence; one must fight. Whoever is silent at such a time is a traitor to humanity."[7]

I present these words to the members of the youth division in particular. One must not remain silent when confronted with acts of inhumanity. Silence amounts to tacit approval. If you are verbally attacked, then counter with ten or twenty times the force. To manifest such a blazing spirit of struggle is the proof of youth.

The French philosopher Henri-Louis Bergson observed that as long as we simply continue advancing, we will draw near our goal. In the process, moreover, we come to recognize that "the so-called obstacles were for the most part the effects of a mirage."[8]

The important thing is that we continue striving to realize our objective. It's true that not to advance is to backslide. When we challenge our circumstances with a strong determination, it suddenly dawns on us that things which had previously seemed onerous and difficult are in fact no big deal at all.

The mind is a wondrous thing. Everything changes completely depending simply on our frame of mind. That is the power and function of the Mystic Law of three thousand realms in a single moment of life.

Maintain a Strong Spirit for Kosen-rufu

The Chinese poet Su Shih said, "Even if someone occupies a lofty place, if his spirit is base, then what can he truly gain?"[9] No matter how high someone's station, what good will it do the person if his or her heart is craven and lowly? Su Shih was not only a poet but also a politician, and his words carry much weight. This certainly goes for leaders in the Soka Gakkai. There is no need for leaders who have lost their spirit for *kosen-rufu* in the Soka Gakkai. I hope your hearts always overflow with a strong passion for *kosen-rufu*.

Also, I want you to be leaders of faith who sincerely respect your fellow members. Those who can respect their comrades in faith will in turn win their respect. This is cause and effect in Buddhism.

New Capable People Open New Avenues

This is the age of youth. Let us genuinely dedicate ourselves to raising fine young leaders. Let us do our best to develop the next generation. By this I don't mean that you should be doting or overly protective. The point is to offer steady training with due strictness and discipline. When new capable people are appointed to positions of leadership, new avenues open up.

At the same time, we also need to treasure those who have worked hard for long years to construct the present foundation. When new leaders and old leaders unite in a spirit of mutual respect, the organization's strength increases many times over.

The Victory of the Women's Division

When facing a strong enemy, youth should play a leading role in efforts to defeat that enemy. But while playing a pivotal role, they must not become arrogant and cause disharmony with the women's division.

As always, our victory at the start of the twenty-first century was due to the victory of the women's division. It is only natural that everyone should respect and appreciate the women's division members and support them so that they can continue to freely and jubilantly carry out activities.

Just because someone has a high standing in the organization or status in society does not mean that person has faith. Someone who behaves arrogantly solely because he or she went to a prestigious school is the worst kind of person and is utterly lacking in character. Some people are flashy; some are modest. Some people have advanced degrees; some don't. Some people are wealthy; some are poor. While all people are different, the important question is who is truly happy.

A person of conviction who leads an upstanding life and demonstrates shining victory in society is a true winner. Put more precisely, a person who has faith is the ultimate victor. Buddhism exists to enable us to lead such a life. This is something that I want to clarify for the sake of the future.

It Is at Times of Adversity That We Must Stand Up in Faith

The Japanese economy continues to be mired in severe recession. No doubt many members are facing difficult circumstances on that account. I hope that as leaders you will show great sensitivity for people's individual situations. At the same time, I want to remind you that no matter how adverse our individual predicament, we need to live out our lives based on steadfast faith. Only then can we accumulate all kinds of treasures in life as true benefit.

Nichiren Daishonin encouraged one of his precious disciples, "You should be willing to offer your life for the Lotus Sutra" (WND-1, 1003). He advised another follower not to "allow concern for your parents, wife, or children to hold you back, or be worried about your property" (WND-1, 764). Nichiren offered this very strict guidance out of his profound compassion for his disciples. It is an expression of austere love.

Faith means limitless hope. Through faith, we can accumulate infinite benefit and create a life of boundless victory. A commentary [by the Great Teacher Dengyo] states, "To discard the shallow and seek the profound is the way of a person of courage" (WND-1, 402). During difficult times, we can overcome hardship through faith and renew our determination to dedicate our lives to *kosen-rufu*. That has been the spirit of the Soka Gakkai since the early days of our movement, and it accords with Nichiren's teaching. Such tenacity of faith and conviction in the power of the Gohonzon generate the strength to overcome any obstacle.

The manner in which President Toda served, respected and protected President Makiguchi was awe-inspiring in every respect. When referring to President Makiguchi, Mr. Toda was the image of solemnity itself.

The mentor-disciple spirit is the soul of the Soka Gakkai. It is the essential path of humanity. Also, putting the members first is the eternal spirit of the Soka Gakkai. We must absolutely never forget this.

Please do everything you can to cause your place of mission to flourish, taking action as a hero of *kosen-rufu* surpassing even the heroes of the Chinese classic *The Romance of the Three Kingdoms*.[10]

From the August 10, 2001, Seikyo Shimbun

NOTES

1 This means negligence in denouncing evil and practicing good, which is one of the fourteen slanders.

2 Israel Epstein, *Woman in World History: Life and Times of Soong Ching Ling (Mme. Sun Yat-sen)* (Beijing: New World Press, 1995), p. 175.

3 Ibid.

4 Translated from Japanese. *Sombun Senshu* (Selected Writings of Sun Yat-sen) vol. 2, edited by Yoshitsugu Ichiji and Ichiro Yamaguchi, translated by Yozo Hayashi (Tokyo: Shakai Shisosha, 1987), p. 308.

5 Translated from French. Victor Hugo, "La Famille Bonaparte," *Actes et Paroles, vol. 1, Avant L'Exil (1841–1851)* (Paris: Albin Michel, 1938), p. 93.

6 Translated from French. Victor Hugo, "Aux Rédacteurs du Rappel," *Actes et Paroles, vol. 3, Depuis L'Exil (1870–1885)* (Paris: Albin Michel, 1940), p. 148.

7 *I Was a German: The Autobiography of Ernst Toller* (New York: William Morrow and Company, 1934), Introduction.

8 Henri Bergson, *Mind-Energy: Lectures and Essays,* translated by H. Wildon Carr (New York: Henry Holt and Company, 1920), pp. 4–5.

9 Translated from Japanese. Mitsuo Kondo, *Chugoku Meishi Kansho, vol. 7: Sotoba* (Appreciation of Chinese Famous Poetry, vol. 7: Su Shih) (Tokyo: Ozawa Shoten, 1996), p. 55.

10 *The Romance of the Three Kingdoms:* An epic saga of three rival kingdoms that fought for control of China in the third century.

Meeting Others Is the Key to Fostering Capable People

AUGUST 2, 2002

In the first half of this year, thanks to the tremendous efforts of you and all the members throughout Japan, we have realized unprecedented development in our movement for *kosen-rufu*. I would like to thank everyone from the bottom of my heart.

If we thoroughly solidify our foundation now, the Soka Gakkai will be secure for all eternity, and *kosen-rufu*—the mission entrusted to us by Nichiren Daishonin—will spread more and more widely around the world. Out of a desire to ensure the eternal development of our movement, I would therefore like to take this opportunity today to reconfirm with you, the leaders of *kosen-rufu*, the fundamental spirit of the Soka Gakkai.

Reaching Out and Forging Heart-to-Heart Ties

As Buddhist leaders, it is vital that we reach out and meet with others. In particular, I hope you will actively make a point of meeting with new members. I say this because Buddhism comes alive in just such human encounters. In his writings, Nichiren emphasized again and again the importance of meeting directly with others.

How can we forge strong personal ties with others? Herein lies the key to development. Indeed, all kinds of business enterprises, organizations and even nations are making every possible effort toward this end.

Meeting others face to face is the only way. Meeting in person forges bonds of trust and brings people together. It also plays a vital role in fostering capable people. Our organization has achieved the global development that it has today precisely because we have persistently carried out such one-to-one dialogue. This is the unwavering formula by which the development of our movement unfolds.

Raising capable people is not achieved through intellectualizing or daydreaming. Second Soka Gakkai president Josei Toda, too, always made a concerted effort to meet people. The Soka Gakkai spirit is found nowhere but in our efforts to meet with and sincerely encourage each person and to advance together toward *kosen-rufu*.

When you take the trouble to go and meet with members, they will feel, "That person cares about me." They will be glad to have seen you and will be inspired to join you in working for *kosen-rufu*.

Also, instead of rushing off immediately after meetings finish, please make time to engage people in conversation, talking with them as you make your way home, for example. There are things that people might not want to share at a big meeting but they might feel free to discuss in private. The fundamental spirit of the Soka Gakkai is found in talking to one another heart to heart and working together for *kosen-rufu*; it is not strategizing or devising grand schemes.

Youth division leaders in particular must not behave arrogantly. I ask the youth leaders to sincerely look after their juniors in faith and work wholeheartedly for the happiness of their fellow members.

Concerning all leaders, there are times when you will be busy with work or family matters, but please still try to make time to meet with others. This is compassion. Such efforts resonate with the behavior of the Buddha. Meeting people is the only way.

Heart-to-heart bonds between people are the very essence of our Buddhist organization, our organization for *kosen-rufu*. If these are lost, the SGI will be reduced to a cold and heartless bureaucracy; it will no longer be a realm of Buddhism.

Don't Grow Complacent; Renew Yourself Each Day!

Someone asked what we can do to help new members gain a thorough grasp of Buddhist doctrine. It is vital that leaders first make an earnest effort to renew their own study of the writings of Nichiren Daishonin. The key is for leaders themselves to read these writings, for them to be inspired and convinced of the correctness of what Nichiren says and then to share those feelings with members. Everything comes down to the leaders.

If leaders don't work to improve or develop themselves, others will not find them attractive or inspiring. Growing complacent and letting Buddhist study slide is a form of arrogance.

Some people have expressed concern that leaders in our organization today don't study Buddhist doctrine as much as their counterparts did in the past. Basing ourselves on the writings of Nichiren is the Soka Gakkai spirit. We must never forget this proud tradition.

There is an ancient Chinese maxim of which first Soka Gakkai president Tsunesaburo Makiguchi was very fond: "Renew yourself each day, day after day after day."

Society is also moving forward day by day, and it is a constant challenge to keep up with the pace of change. Apathy is the path to defeat. The bureaucratic mentality that tends to take root in organizations is the source of all evils.

Leadership positions are not an empty formality; they are positions of responsibility. For example, train engineers are entrusted with the lives of their passengers. They have a responsibility to protect them, even at the risk of their own lives, from the start of the journey to its end. What would happen if train engineers didn't pay any attention and just gazed at the passing scenery the whole time? Leaders are the engineers, and the organization is the train. When the engineers conscientiously fulfill their duties, the train will advance safely toward its destination.

Leaders must be the first to stand up. I would like all of you here at this conference to take the initiative.

Also, when attending discussion meetings, it is important that you, as leaders, make it your personal responsibility to foster each and every individual there for the sake of *kosen-rufu* and the eternal perpetuation of the Law. Please encourage them with all your heart, having faith that each one will grow into a person of great mission who can manifest the ability and strength of several hundreds or thousands of people.

Undertaking the Buddha's Work

The SGI's goal is to actualize *kosen-rufu*; it is for each individual to achieve true happiness. President Toda frequently said: "We of the Soka Gakkai, who are undertaking the Buddha's work of leading the suffering to happiness, receive benefit without the slightest doubt. That is why I continually call on you to staunchly protect our organization."[1]

The SGI seeks to enable all people to realize genuine, indestructible happiness, not only those who are obviously suffering but also those who are leading what appear to be happy and enjoyable lives. That is because, no matter how happy individuals may think they are, there is no happiness greater than practicing Nichiren Buddhism. As the Daishonin said, "There is no true happiness for human beings other than chanting Nam-myoho-renge-kyo" (WND-1, 681). The SGI organization is the sole realm of correct Buddhist practice that enables us to attain a state of absolute happiness. That is why President Toda enjoined us to protect our organization.

An organization is like a person's frame. Having a strong frame is important for healthy growth and development. In the same way, when the organization is united and solid, its members are protected and *kosen-rufu* can advance.

Exerting Ten Times Our Present Effort

President Toda also said, "When we are joined by many young people who have faith in and practice the great Buddhism of Nichiren Daishonin, we can definitely accomplish *kosen-rufu*."[2] If young people gather, we can definitely achieve *kosen-rufu*—the youth division must never forget these words of Mr. Toda.

Youth should have the spirit to exert ten times the effort they have up to now. Faith is not empty posturing or lip service. It is action. It is all about whether you can stand up alone.

I fought with my entire being alongside Mr. Toda for the sake of *kosen-rufu*. Taking on full responsibility for the Soka Gakkai, I traveled around the country and exerted myself without rest. I was ready to give my life for Mr. Toda, if need be. That is why I won in all struggles and created history.

Mr. Toda also said, "The Gakkai's strength, ultimately, is that it is supported by young people."[3] Youth are the power, life and hope of the Gakkai. The Soka Gakkai must forever be a youthful organization.

I would like our youth division members of the twenty-first century to champion lofty ideals. I dedicate these words from Mr. Toda to you: "I want you to be fine young people who cherish the ideal of benefiting the nation, while at the same time making efforts in your immediate environment to solidify your own foundations."[4]

Speak Out Unsparingly To Share the Correct Teaching of Buddhism

What is the correct practice for us as practitioners of Nichiren Buddhism in modern times? It is *shakubuku*. The Daishonin repeatedly emphasized that *shakubuku* is the practice suited to the Latter Day of the Law. In "On Practicing the Buddha's Teachings," he wrote:

> Now, in the Latter Day of the Law, who is carrying out the practice of *shakubuku* in strict accordance with the Lotus Sutra? Suppose someone, no matter whom, should unrelentingly proclaim that the Lotus Sutra alone can lead people to Buddhahood, and that all other sutras, far from enabling them to attain the way, only drive them into hell. Observe what happens should that person thus try to refute the teachers and the doctrines of all the other schools. The three powerful enemies will arise without fail. (WND-1, 394)

"Speak out unsparingly to share the correct teaching of Buddhism with others!" —this is the Daishonin's admonition to us.

President Makiguchi said: "Propagation is the essence of religion. A life devoted to benefiting others represents great good."[5] He also said, "A coward who cannot speak out and say what must be said cannot be a disciple of the Daishonin."

Meanwhile, President Toda declared: "It's not good to lead a life bound by the chains of suffering. Chanting Nam-myoho-renge-kyo and *shakubuku* constitute the sharp sword that can cut through those chains. The mission and spirit of the Soka Gakkai are to enable all our fellow citizens to attain a state of life unfettered by the chains of suffering."[6]

We of the Soka Gakkai, armed with courage and a lionlike spirit, have undertaken the practice of *shakubuku* in accord with the teachings of the Daishonin and the guidance of Mr. Makiguchi and Mr. Toda.

The Nikken sect, in contrast, does not do *shakubuku*, and where the *shakubuku* spirit does not exist, we cannot possibly hope to find the spirit of Nichiren Daishonin, the Buddha of the Latter Day of the Law. Bereft of the essential spirit of faith, the Nikken sect is a dead religion. It allowed itself to grow corrupt and decadent. In doing so, it sullied the pure flow of faith and degenerated into a slanderous Buddhist school.

The Purpose of Religion

Centuries ago, Nichiren's successor, Nikko Shonin, left Mount Minobu, which had become a place of slander of the Law. He wrote, "Irrespective of where I may go, the most important thing is correctly passing on the Daishonin's teachings and spreading them in society" (Hennentai Gosho,[7] p. 1733).

The Soka Gakkai also parted ways with the head temple, which had turned into a center of slander of the Law. Dedicated to carrying out the Buddha's decree, we have significantly advanced the *kosen-rufu* movement throughout the world.

I am firmly convinced that these events have all unfolded according to Nichiren's intentions. Mr. Makiguchi once said: "We're trying to faithfully carry out the Daishonin's decree, so what could possibly be holding you back? Buddhism is not an intellectual game. Its purpose is to liberate the land and the people from suffering. To stand by with folded arms and fail to do so when the time arises is to betray the Buddha's intent."

He also asked, "What is the social raison d'être of religion apart from working for the happiness of humanity and making the world a better place?"

Nichiren Buddhism teaches the most right and proper practice for human beings. When doing what is good and right, there is no need to hesitate or be afraid.

Let us advance with optimism, joy and confidence along the path of realizing peace and prosperity in society based on the ideals and principles of Buddhism, along the path of world peace, just as the Daishonin instructs.

From the August 6, 2002, Seikyo Shimbun

Notes

1 Josei Toda, *Toda Josei zenshu* (Collected Writings of Josei Toda), vol. 4, p. 44.
2 Ibid., p. 150.
3 Ibid., p. 241.
4 Ibid., p. 404.
5 Kikuo Ichikawa, *Makiguchi Tsunesaburo sensei no omoide* (Memories of Tsunesaburo Makiguchi) (Fukuoka, Japan: Seikyo Shimbunsha Kyushu Editorial Bureau, 1976), p. 58.
6 Cf. *Josei Toda zenshu*, vol. 4, p. 180.

7 Abbreviation of *Hennentai Nichiren Daishonin gosho*: The chronological Japanese-language compilation of Nichiren Daishonin's writings published by the Soka Gakkai in 1974. It also includes two letters by Nikko Shonin ("Reply to Mimasaka-bo" and "Reply to Lord Hara").

Aim Higher, Higher Still!

AUGUST 2, 2002

Realizing a peaceful land through the propagation of the correct teaching [*rissho ankoku*]—this was the wish of Nichiren Daishonin. Land, here, doesn't mean the single nation of Japan. Twenty-sixth high priest Nichikan said it refers to Jambudvipa—the entire world—and to the future. In other words, the Daishonin aspired to everlasting world peace.

Today, in North and South America, in Asia, in Oceania, in Europe, in Africa—in 183 countries and territories[1] around the world—fellow Bodhisattvas of the Earth are energetically carrying out SGI activities.

In India, the cradle of Buddhism, SGI members are making wonderful contributions to society. The spacious Soka Bodhi Tree Garden [located in Gurgaon, south of New Delhi] resembles the beautiful grove of jeweled trees mentioned in the Lotus Sutra (cf. LS16, 230).

We are making the westward transmission of Buddhism a reality.

Victory Comes From Prayer

What determines the true worth of a leader? It is not popularity or outward appearances but how earnestly a leader serves the people. True worth is determined by a leader's commitment and actions to this end.

Leaders must possess a philosophy—a correct philosophy that contributes to human happiness and leads people toward peace.

We of the SGI possess the wonderful humanistic philosophy of the Mystic Law. We are practicing the Mystic Law ourselves and teaching it to many others. We are leaders without rival in the world.

The famous French writer Victor Hugo once declared that all great people were the target of abuse.

Yet precisely because we champion the cause of good, it is vital that we triumph! Just wait and see our final victory! This is the spirit of indomitable champions of truth.

Victory starts with earnest prayer, with a vow based on the spirit of oneness of mentor and disciple.

To forever protect and continue to develop this noble and magnificent organization of the Buddha's emissaries that is the Soka Gakkai, to give our all for *kosen-rufu*—this is the spirit with which we should advance as leaders.

Women Are the Sun of Our Movement

Mothers are the sun of the family, and the women's division is the sun of the Soka Gakkai. Women are a brilliant light imparting courage to their friends and spreading hope in society. I ask that our male leaders sincerely respect and value the women's division members.

Realizing Our True Mission

During his wartime imprisonment—the result of persecution by the militarist authorities—second Soka Gakkai president Josei Toda awoke to the realization that he himself was a Bodhisattva of the Earth. Through that experience, he came to declare, "The essence of human revolution is attaining the state of life where, from the very depths of one's being, one is free of doubts and delusions about life and realizes one's true mission."[2]

This "true mission" is none other than *kosen-rufu*, the ultimate goal of our Buddhist practice.

Mr. Toda called on the youth to dedicate their lives to this mission, proclaiming:

> I believe that it is vital for youth who are truly concerned for the welfare of the nation and who wish for the happiness of the people to themselves earnestly seek the essence of this lofty human revolution and advance bravely and vigorously, fighting and triumphing over all manifestations of the "three powerful enemies" and the "three obstacles and four devils."[3]

In the course of our efforts to widely spread the correct teaching of Buddhism, it is only to be expected that the three powerful enemies and the three obstacles and four devils will make their appearance. That is the time when youth should loudly proclaim the justice of our cause, when they should let forth a mighty lion's roar. "Advancing bravely and vigorously" should be the perennial spirit of the Soka Gakkai youth division.

"A Hundred Reforms Will All Be in Vain"

Soka Gakkai founding president Tsunesaburo Makiguchi sternly denounced the injustice of upright and honest people being persecuted and maligned: "Unless we fundamentally eliminate this deplorable situation where jealous individuals are able to undermine and oust their rivals—no matter how small such an incident may be—a hundred reforms will all be in vain."[4] He called on us to recognize even the smallest instance of injustice, for unless such abuses were completely nipped in the bud, all our efforts would come to naught. This was Mr. Makiguchi's conviction.

Mr. Makiguchi also said, "Removing evil elements is essential to securing a peaceful existence for the majority of a community's members."[5] I hope you will never become the kind of cowardly individuals who gaze on indifferently while wrongdoing is perpetrated, taking the attitude that it doesn't concern you and that getting involved will only be to your detriment—the kind of self-serving individuals who constantly try to make themselves look good and maneuver to protect themselves from becoming the target of attack. Indifference to injustice is our enemy. Those who pretend not to see evil are accomplices to evil.

Lies, no matter how small, that malign and discredit the just must not go unchallenged. It is crucial that we thoroughly expose all malicious false propaganda and defamatory statements for what they are by speaking out vigorously in the spirit of "refuting the erroneous and revealing the true." Especially when youth rise to this challenge, the integrity and goodness of society as a whole will be protected.

"Suffering Is a Necessary Condition for Growth"

The famous German philosopher Arthur Schopenhauer said, "Envy of others is an indicator of how unhappy people are with themselves."[6] The envious are sad, unhappy individuals.

A famous saying by the Russian writer Leo Tolstoy is "Suffering is the necessary condition for spiritual and physical growth."[7]

Experiencing various trials and problems leads to personal growth and to the polishing of our character. In particular, all of our challenges and exertions in working to realize *kosen-rufu* make our lives sparkle like gemstones. This is a principle of Buddhism.

John Milton, the renowned English poet, wrote, "Who best can suffer, best can do."[8]

Allow me to share more of Mr. Toda's words with you: "The fundamental philosophy is the philosophy of life. We are leading the world with a great philosophy one step higher [than capitalism and communism]."[9]

We have truly entered the age in which the great life philosophy of Buddhism will lead the world. Many thoughtful, discerning leaders around the globe are focusing intently on the wisdom of Buddhism and enthusiastically endorse the humanistic principles upheld by the SGI.

Let us proudly work to expand our network dedicated to bringing peace to the world through the propagation of the correct teaching of Buddhism.

Mr. Makiguchi said, "Toward greater and ever greater perfection—this is our desire in all things."[10] Aim higher! Higher still! Buddhism gives us wings to soar to limitless self-improvement.

From the August 7, 2002, Seikyo Shimbun

Notes

1 As of the publication of this book, the number of countries and territories where SGI members practice Nichiren Buddhism is 192.

2 *Toda Josei zenshu* (Collected Writings of Josei Toda), vol. 1, p. 266.

3 Ibid., p. 267.

4 *Makiguchi Tsunesaburo zenshu* (Collected Writings of Tsunesaburo Makiguchi), vol. 6, p. 178.

5 Ibid., vol. 9, p. 99.

6 Translated from German. Arthur Schopenhauer, *Aphorismen zur Lebensweisheit* (Counsels and Maxims), edited by Arthur Hübscher (Stuttgart: Philipp Reclam Jun, 1968), p. 170.

7 Leo Tolstoy, *A Calendar of Wisdom: Wise Thoughts for Every Day*, translated by Peter Sekirin (London: Hodder & Stoughton, 1997), p. 164.

8 John Milton, *The Works of John Milton* (New York: Columbia University Press, 1959), vol. 2, p. 449. ("Paradise Regain'd," ll. 194–95.)

9 *Toda Josei zenshu*, vol. 4, pp. 28–29.

10 *Makiguchi Tsunesaburo zenshu*, vol. 6, p. 92.

Toward a World of Peace and Happiness for All Humanity

AUGUST 2, 2002

It is the spirit of youth division members to protect their mentor and to stand up to take full responsibility for *kosen-rufu*.

In my youth, I stood up alone to take on the full brunt of all onslaughts by authoritarian forces that sought to oppress our movement—most specifically, the injustices of the Yubari Coal Miners Union Incident and the Osaka Incident [which both took place in 1957].[1]

I unequivocally assured my mentor, Mr. Toda, who was deeply concerned about the situation: "Sensei, please don't worry. I have everything under control. Please rest easy." And he always used to say happily, "Thanks to Daisaku, I can rest easy."

Mr. Toda was a towering leader of *kosen-rufu*. My mind was solely filled with thoughts of how to protect him, how to go about realizing his vision and how to communicate his greatness to people around the world.

In 1996, I gave a lecture[2] at Columbia University's Teachers College, one of the leading schools of education in the United States, on Soka value-creating education, which was developed by Mr. Makiguchi and his disciple Mr. Toda. On that occasion, I was asked about Soka University of America, and I shared my hopes that the university would produce people who would lead the twenty-first and twenty-second centuries based on the pillars of peace, human rights and the sanctity of life.

I have actualized, down to the letter, the vision cherished by my mentor for the creation of a great path of education, peace and culture. The entire heart and essence of the Soka Gakkai can be found in this spirit of mentor and disciple. This is our solemn history. I wish to proclaim this for the sake of future generations.

Don't Be Dependent on Others

Today, the Soka Gakkai's stage is the world. The path has been opened. The rest is up to the youth. Now is the time for the youth to train and develop themselves in earnest.

Looking back on the early days of our movement, I remember us youth division members literally running from the train station to attend Gakkai meetings after work. That's the kind of enthusiasm and energy we had.

Young people shouldn't be too easy on themselves, because that is the path to ruin. Cast aside your dependency! There is no way but to stand up in faith through your own efforts. With your sincere and persistent prayers, please touch the lives of all around you—friends and opponents alike—and create a grand alliance of the people and a powerful new groundswell for *kosen-rufu*.

The Young Women's Division Is the Key

Mr. Toda's dearest wish was for each member of the young women's division to become happy without a single exception.

The young women's division is important. I wish to foster the young women's division. If one resolute woman stands up, she can illuminate all around her with the brilliant light of hope. If the young women's division develops, the Soka Gakkai will shine and the future of *kosen-rufu* will open wide.

Let us all chant for the great development of the young women's division and do everything we can to support and encourage them.

Everything Starts From Our Inner Resolve

It is vital to continually breathe fresh air and fresh energy into our organization, which is dedicated to widely propagating the teachings of Buddhism.

Each of our members has a profound mission for *kosen-rufu*. How can we enable them to bring forth their full potential? How can we best advance *kosen-rufu* in a way that protects everyone and brings them joy? It is the responsibility of leaders to concentrate all their energies on these points and work hard behind the scenes to support their fellow members.

What we need to do is boldly give leadership responsibility to people of ability and potential, build a strong central core, work to unite people's hearts and advance in the spirit of "many in body, one in mind." Newly appointed leaders also need to make even greater efforts for *kosen-rufu* than before. I hope they will actively go out and meet and talk with many people with the goal of transforming their communities or regions into ideal realms of peace and happiness for all.

Nichiren said, "From this single element of mind spring all the various lands and environmental conditions" (WND-2, 843). As the principle of "three thousand realms in a single moment of life" teaches, the power to transform society lies in the fundamental attitude or inner resolve of human beings.

It's not up to others; it all comes down to us. Our inner resolve and our actions have a more powerful influence than a book of a million words. Through taking action, we will also feel a sense of purpose and savor joy and good fortune.

Speak Out Against Injustice!

The spirit of refuting error and denouncing evil is the essence of Buddhism. It is also the Soka Gakkai spirit.

In his treatise "On Establishing the Correct Teaching for the Peace of the Land," Nichiren clearly states the cause of disasters that befall the nation and the misfortunes that afflict its people, "The people of today all turn their backs upon what is right; to a person, they give their allegiance to evil" (WND-1, 7). He goes on to say, "I cannot keep silent on this matter" (WND-1, 7). With this spirit, he remonstrated with the highest authorities of the day.

The youth division, too, must have the ability to vehemently denounce wrongdoing.

"How dare anyone spread malicious lies that tear down good, decent people!" Driven by such thunderous anger toward injustice, we must expose, thoroughly condemn and eliminate such evils. Only then can we call ourselves true champions of justice.

Mr. Makiguchi remarked to the effect: "People of minor good resembling a flock of sheep stand by idly while the just are viciously persecuted by the insolent acts of evil people. This represents a grave future peril for our nation." Don't become a flock of sheep, afraid to speak out when the time demands. Don't be people of minor good, for their presence endangers the nation's future. This was Mr. Makiguchi's clarion call. And, just as he warned, Japan, which was then under the rule of a militarist government, advanced headlong down the path to self-destruction. This is an undeniable historical fact.

Global Journey for Peace and Culture

Thomas Jefferson, the third U.S. president, observed that people's labors would quickly transform the whole earth into a paradise were it not for misgovernment or the tendency for people's energies to be diverted from the proper goal of human happiness and directed instead to the selfish interests of kings, nobles and priests.[3]

I am firmly convinced that the SGI's momentous global journey for peace and culture will take us with absolute certainty to an ideal realm of happiness and prosperity for all people.

The ancient Greek philosopher Plato wrote in *The Republic* that a person without character cannot attain self-contentment merely by the attainment of riches.[4] What truly matters is not wealth, social status or fame; rather, it is our character and humanity. And what enables us to develop our character and humanity is our Buddhist practice.

There Is No Retirement Age in Buddhism

Shakyamuni Buddha and Nichiren Daishonin continued their struggles to propagate the Law right up to the very end of their lives.

The Daishonin wrote: "Life is limited; we must not begrudge it. What we should ultimately aspire to is the Buddha land" (WND-1, 214). There is no retirement age in Buddhism. And there is no retirement from life. We must continue working all our lives, to our hearts' content, for the sake of people's happiness and for the sake of the Law. If we take ourselves away from Gakkai activities, our lives will only be empty and lonely. We must proceed to the end on the path of *kosen-rufu* that we have chosen to walk in this lifetime.

Buddhism teaches the oneness of birth and death. It is important that we bring our lives to a magnificent close, just like the setting sun paints the sky in majestic crimson hues.

The truly great do not seek greatness for themselves; they seek to enable others to realize greatness. It is the responsibility of seniors to protect and work for the welfare of their juniors and to foster them so that they can become even more capable than themselves.

Forever Expanding Our Network of Kosen-rufu

Mr. Makiguchi first took faith in the teachings of Nichiren Daishonin in 1928 at age fifty-seven. After doing so, he encountered various persecutions, just as the Lotus Sutra and Nichiren's writings predict. Some of his friends coldly deserted him. But he also wrote that due to embracing Nichiren Buddhism, he was blessed with many new friends: "As a result of embracing faith, I have had the opportunity to meet some extraordinary people, and, unworthy though I am, I have made more than a hundred new close friends whom I encouraged to reform their lives."[5]

As long as he lived, Mr. Makiguchi continued to increase his circle of comrades in faith and to develop his state of life limitlessly by taking action for *kosen-rufu*, chanting Nam-myoho-renge-kyo and writing and speaking to spread the Law. This ceaseless dedication is the way of life of Buddhism; it is the way of life of Soka.

As we enter the remaining few months of the Year of Expanding Dialogue [2002], let us widen our circle of new members even further and joyfully open another triumphant page in the annals of our movement!

From the August 8, 2002, Seikyo Shimbun

Notes

1 Yubari Coal Miners Union Incident: In 1957, a case of religious discrimination in which miners in Yubari, Hokkaido, were threatened with losing their jobs because they belonged to the Soka Gakkai. President Ikeda, then Soka Gakkai youth division chief of staff, went to Hokkaido to support the members in their struggle against this injustice. Osaka Incident: President Ikeda, then Soka Gakkai youth division chief of staff, was arrested and jailed on July 3, 1957, on trumped-up charges of election law violations in a by-election in Osaka. He was released two weeks later on July 17. In January 1962, at the end of a lengthy trial, he was fully exonerated of all charges.

2 The lecture, made at the college's invitation, was titled, "Thoughts on Education for Global Citizenship."

3 Ralph Ketcham, *From Colony to Country—The Revolution in American Thought, 1750–1820* (New York: Macmillan Publishing Co., Inc., 1974), p. 277.

4 Plato, *The Republic, Books I–V*, translated by Paul Shorey (Cambridge, MA: Harvard University Press, 1994), p. 15.

5 *Makiguchi Tsunesaburo zenshu* (Collected Writings of Tsunesaburo Makiguchi), vol. 8, p. 15.

Make Your Way Confidently

"Don't be ruled by fear. Make your way confidently! Let the Gakkai always advance confidently!" This was Mr. Toda's injunction.

We must never forget to have the spirit to refute the erroneous and reveal the true. By the same token, however, leaders of our organization must never be haughty or arrogant toward their fellow members. Only the worst leader would act in such a way. I hope that you will be courageous and strong when it comes to fighting injustice and dealing with attacks from without.

"The voice carries out the work of the Buddha" (WND-2, 57). Our voice can serve as a jeweled sword for cutting down evil and corruption, or it can express warm, heartfelt encouragement. The voice that does the Buddha's work is not merely our physical voice; it is also the words we write in proclaiming and defending the truth. There are people filled with malice and ill intent. We cannot allow their vicious lies and outrageous claims to go unchallenged. There are members and friends who are suffering. We need to reach out to them with words of support and encouragement. It is important to respond immediately to the issues before us. Remaining silent is foolish, lacking in compassion and leads to defeat.

Simple words of kindness and appreciation—"Thank you for

coming from so far away," "I really appreciate your efforts," or "Let's create something memorable"—can spread joy and happiness to others. It will allow everyone to advance with confidence and peace of mind.

Small incremental efforts can lead to great victory in life. The same principle applies to our struggle for *kosen-rufu*. One-on-one dialogue sets the giant wheel of history in motion.

The Spirit of Mentor and Disciple Is the Spirit of Soka

The fate of all organizations is decided by their first three generations of leaders. Founding president Tsunesaburo Makiguchi, second president Josei Toda and I, as the third president inheriting the spirit of my two predecessors, built the foundations of our organization. Mr. Toda solemnly said to me: "You are the third president. Lead the *kosen-rufu* movement throughout your life. I leave the Gakkai completely in your hands." I staunchly supported Mr. Toda and threw my whole being into building the Soka Gakkai into the foremost organization it is in Japan and the world today.

Mr. Toda once firmly instructed the youth division, "If the members all support the third president, *kosen-rufu* will surely be achieved."[1] If the Soka Gakkai remains based on the spirit of mentor and disciple that was shared by its first, second and third presidents, its future triumph is assured. This is the sole source for the everlasting growth and development of our organization. I would like to make this point absolutely clear for the sake of the future.

Cast Aside Airs and Pretension

The twenty-first century is the century of the youth division. The full-fledged ascent of the lofty summit of *kosen-rufu* lies before you.

There is no grander stage on which to live out your youth than that of the Soka Gakkai. There is no stage of endeavor more wonderful, both from the perspective of its underlying philosophy and its international scope. If you don't leave behind a great history now, when will you?

As youth, it is important that you devote yourselves earnestly and sincerely to *kosen-rufu*, whether others are watching your efforts or not. Please cast aside airs and pretension. Putting on airs is pathetic playacting. With pretense, you can't help others. You can't even make yourself happy. Nichiren wrote, "Rely on the Law and not upon persons" (WND-1, 872). The important thing is that we devote our lives to the Mystic Law.

If, in our earnest endeavor to promote this great people's movement for *kosen-rufu*, you behave as if everything's a joke or strut about with self-centered arrogance, you will destroy the noble realm of Buddhism. If you forget the demanding practice of faith and just seek to enjoy an easy, indolent life, hellish suffering is bound to await you down the line. Nichiren sternly warned us of this in his writings.

Hard work is a priceless treasure for young people. Instead of putting on a performance to try to win popularity, please strive with all your might to fight the enemies of Buddhism, protect your fellow members and open the way for the triumph of *kosen-rufu*. Only through such genuine hard work will you earn the trust and confidence of the members of the women's and men's divisions.

The Importance of Unity

Allow me now to share the sayings of some eminent world figures. My reason for doing so is that the wise words of great thinkers of the past can serve as a source of illumination for us in our efforts to overcome hardship and live lives of truth and justice.

Members of Bharat Soka Gakkai [SGI-India] in the state of Himachal-Pradesh have sent me some words Mahatma Gandhi wrote while he was visiting their region.

Gandhi said, "Untruth corrodes the soul; truth nourishes it."[2] Deceit corrupts the spirit and fosters human misery. Truth enriches our spirit and fosters human happiness. That is why it is so important to thoroughly expose falsehoods and work to spread the truth.

Gandhi also said, "If a man has a living faith in him, it spreads its aroma like the rose its scent."[3] A "living faith" lies not in abstract concepts or commandments; it is found in action and in practice. It means that our conduct is the embodiment of our faith.

And speaking of the importance of unity, the great Indian champion of nonviolence said:

> But I do not want unity on paper. If we write out a pact on paper, unity is not thereby achieved. The unity I want is the unity of heart and for that unity I always pray. And when that unity is achieved you will gain such strength as will give us success.[4]

No matter how many fine words we may string together, they alone cannot produce unity or lead to victory. Unity comes from hearts joined together. The spirit of "many in body, one in mind" forms the basis for true unity.

Stand Alone! Others Are Sure To Follow!

Gandhi emphatically declared, "Ahimsa [nonviolence] is one of the world's great principles which no power on earth can wipe out."[5] Gandhi rose up alone to spread the philosophy of nonviolence. He proved the maxim that if one courageous individual stands up, he or she can change the world.

Gandhi asserted that even if there were one pure person in a gathering, the rest would be affected by that one person's purity.[6] The presence of one person is important. If one person stands up, two, three and more are certain to follow his or her example. Those who can stand alone possess true courage and are genuine leaders.

The Vital Role of Women

President Makiguchi, in *The System of Value-Creating Education* [*Soka kyoikugaku taikei*], called attention to the Swedish thinker and educator Ellen Key. The words of this pioneering feminist, who strove to improve the position of women in society some one hundred years ago, shine with even greater brilliance today.

Key wrote, "No profound spiritual transformation has ever taken place unless women have taken part in it."[7] She also said, "If women are to give the development of society a direction wholly different from that which man has given it, this will depend on the appearance among women of leaders who shall point the way to higher aims and employ purer means."[8]

The new century is one in which the wisdom of women will truly shine. It is the century in which women will stand up to play an increasingly active role. And those organizations, companies and nations where women can speak out freely on any subject and dynamically actualize their potential will experience growth and prosperity. That is why it is so important for men to value women and their contributions.

Key also wrote, "New conditions arise above all through new

human beings, new souls, new emotions."[9] I hope that the members of our women's and young women's divisions will create a new age with fresh spirits and fresh emotions.

I'd also like to share these words of Florence Nightingale with our women's and young women's divisions' members, "I have never repented nor looked back, not for one moment."[10]

Toward a Fresh Round of Victories

The great champion of the American civil rights movement, Dr. Martin Luther King Jr., declared, "Religion endows us with the conviction that we are not alone in this vast, uncertain universe."[11] True religion teaches the basic principles of the universe; it teaches the eternity of life and a firm purpose for living. If we understand the true essence of life, we will never suffer from a sense of being alone in this universe.

Thomas Jefferson, the third president of the United States, wrote, "The whole art of government consists in the art of being honest."[12] Honesty is crucial; the honest person triumphs in life. The higher one's position, the more important honesty is. This is the mark of a truly humanistic organization.

Let me once again share the words of Ellen Key with you. She declared that we need "courage for our own destiny, courage to bear it or break under it, and also courage to wait for, to choose our destiny."[13] Faith is courage. Cowardice is defeat. Those armed with courage are unbeatable.

Key asserted that the victorious are usually those who have answered in the affirmative the inner question of whether they will triumph.[14] The person who decides to win will win. The person who is strongly determined to be victorious will be victorious.

With that strength of spirit, let us embark anew toward a fresh round of victories!

From the August 9, 2002, Seikyo Shimbun

Notes

1 At a youth division study session held on February 17, 1952.
2 Mahatma Gandhi, *The Collected Works of Mahatma Gandhi* (Ahmedabad: Publications Division, Ministry of Information and Broadcasting, Government of India), vol. 80 (April 25–July 16, 1945), p. 437.
3 Ibid., vol. 46 (April 16–June 17, 1931), p. 28.
4 Ibid., p. 152.
5 Ibid., vol. 84 (April 14–July 15, 1946), p. 127.
6 Ibid., vol. 80 (April 25–July 16, 1945), p. 378.
7 Ellen Key, *Love and Marriage*, translated by Arthur G. Chapter (New York: G. P. Putnam's Sons, 1911), p. 260.
8 Ibid., p. 249.
9 Ibid., p. 259.
10 Edward Cook, *The Life of Florence Nightingale* (London: MacMillan and Co., Limited, 1913), vol. 1, p. 138.
11 Martin Luther King Jr., *Strength to Love* (Philadelphia: Fortress Press, 1981), p. 123.
12 Thomas Jefferson, *A Summary View of the Rights of British America* (New York: Scholars' Facsimiles & Reprints, 1943), pp. 22–23.
13 Cf. Ellen Key, *Love and Marriage*, p. 194.
14 Ibid., p. 280.

Laying the Foundations for Victory One Hundred Years Ahead

How can we triumph in the next fifty years? How can we achieve great progress in the next hundred years? I am always praying earnestly, thinking hard and training people to ensure that the Soka Gakkai, with its mission of *kosen-rufu*, will develop forever and enjoy a bright, shining future.

As leaders, it is essential that we cultivate the strength never to be defeated by anything. The starting point for this is the mentor-disciple spirit. Everything hinges on us challenging our own reformation each day, so that we grow more today than yesterday and more tomorrow than today. We as leaders must elevate our life-condition.

There are certain to be momentous obstacles on the road to *kosen-rufu*. To triumph over them and protect our precious members, let us build a solid force of capable people to lead our movement.

Life Is Not Defined by Age

Soka Gakkai activities allow us to accumulate great good fortune. Our bonds with our fellow members last a lifetime, indeed, for all eternity.

Our illustrious predecessor, first Soka Gakkai president Tsune-saburo Makiguchi, declared, "Whatever one's age, a person who keeps growing day after day is young." How old we are does not define our life.

No matter how young we are in years, if we lack a fighting spirit, we are old. We mustn't take a step back or withdraw from the struggle. If we actively keep working for *kosen-rufu* wherever we go, if we keep our passion for *kosen-rufu* blazing brightly in our hearts whatever our age, then we are young.

President Makiguchi observed: "The Daishonin wrote, 'Buddhism primarily concerns itself with victory or defeat, while secular authority is based on the principle of reward and punishment' (WND-1, 835). These words are indeed the very lifeblood of Nichiren Buddhism."

Buddhism is concerned with victory or defeat. Secular authority is concerned with reward and punishment. Society, sadly, is swayed by rumor and gossip. The essence of Nichiren Buddhism is whether we win or lose in our actual lives. Let us all be victorious in life without fail.

Leaders Have a Responsibility To Speak Up for What Is Right

Mr. Makiguchi also declared, "What social raison d'être could a religion possibly have apart from leading people and society toward enlightenment?" This is indeed a bold statement. Let us call out just as boldly for truth and justice.

Mr. Makiguchi sternly warned, "Do not be cowards who fail to say what needs to be said and later regret it."

It is especially deplorable when people in positions of responsibility do not speak up for what is right. Their inaction contributes to evil and also harms their own lives. They will end up being afraid to speak up for anything and will lead a life filled with regrets.

It is essential that we wage a struggle based on courageous speech and win. Our voice does the Buddha's work. Our voice advances *kosen-rufu*. Our voice serves as the shining sword for refuting the erroneous and revealing the true.

Mr. Makiguchi commented: "People of small good who lack the courage to do great good cannot be counted on for much. . . . They are completely useless when powerful adversaries appear, and their behavior causes people to lose trust in one another." We need to have courage to take action for the sake of great good. We must have that strength of character.

The Greek dramatist Aeschylus wrote, "Thanks to our duel for [goodness]; we win through it all."[1] We will win because our struggle is for the sake of good; indeed, for that very reason, we must win.

Aeschylus also wrote, "There is no infamy I more despise [than the treachery of those who desert their friends]."[2] No one is more loathed or despised than a traitor, he says.

The Roman statesman and author Cicero, meanwhile, was of the opinion that "No duty is more imperative than that of proving one's gratitude."[3] These words express a view of life very similar to that of Buddhism.

Trust Is the Greatest Treasure for Youth

Allow me to change the subject. I have heard that some of my words were carried in the *Hankook Ilbo*, one of South Korea's four major newspapers, in a column titled "Koh Do-won's Morning Reflections."

[*"Koh Do-won's Morning Reflections"* is a popular daily front-page column by Koh Do-won, a former secretary to the president of South Korea, in which he presents an inspiring quote or maxim along with a brief personal commentary.]

The column introduced some remarks I made on the subject of trust as follows:

> Trust is hard to establish but easy to lose. The trust that it has taken a decade to build can be destroyed by a seemingly minor word or action at a crucial moment. . . .
>
> People who take pride in their work, humble and inconspicuous as it may be, and who persevere step by step to make themselves better people, build genuine trust.

For young people, such trust is the greatest treasure. This is one of the lessons in life that I learned from my mentor, President Toda.

Dramatic Strides in Publications Promotion

Through the all-out efforts of our members around Japan in the first half of the year, we achieved a dramatic expansion in the readership of the *Seikyo Shimbun*, the Soka Gakkai's daily newspaper. I am deeply grateful for everyone's efforts.

President Toda regarded the propagation of Nichiren Buddhism and the expansion of the *Seikyo Shimbun*'s readership as the two wheels of *kosen-rufu*. They may not be glamorous activities, but they are the most important driving forces of *kosen-rufu*.

Mr. Toda asserted that the *Seikyo Shimbun* is a powerful weapon in our struggle to propagate Nichiren Buddhism. In this age, when many are decrying the decline in reading, the mission of the *Seikyo Shimbun* takes on even greater importance. Let us continue to make a vigorous effort in the second half of the year to expand the *Seikyo*

Shimbun's readership still further as a means to promote peace, culture and education.

The Age of the Youth Division

The age of the youth division is now well and truly here. I am committed to treasuring our youth above all and to watching over their growth and development.

The times are moving very swiftly. If we don't pass the baton on to new people in every area of our movement in the next few years, we will be left behind.

Mr. Toda bequeathed us this important guidance, "Unless our youth become great in every field of endeavor, we cannot hope to accomplish *kosen-rufu.*"

Winning People's Hearts

The French writer André Maurois offered the following keen observation, "A great leader is a great character; he is unbiased and without self-interest."[4] Each of you is a leader of *kosen-rufu.* Each of you has a huge mission.

I'd like to share several basic principles relating to the art of leadership, which I learned from Mr. Toda in my youth.

What is the most important quality for a leader?

Mr. Toda said, "If you aren't trusted and respected by the members, you won't be able to succeed in guiding them in faith." Leaders must win by gaining people's trust—this was Mr. Toda's conclusion. Inspiring the members' trust and behaving with utmost sincerity and integrity are vital for leaders.

It is also important that leaders listen carefully to what everyone has to say. Instead of talking all the time, leaders need to be considerate of others and show respect for others' feelings; they should make a point of asking people their opinions and inquiring whether there is anything that might be troubling them. Such leaders win people's hearts.

The Philosophy of Leadership in the Soka Gakkai

President Toda often used the example of the ancient Chinese hero Chuko K'ung-ming [also known as Zhuge Liang] from *The Romance of the Three Kingdoms*[5] to give us important guidance.

I will never forget these words of K'ung-ming: "Leaders are responsible for people's lives. On them hinges success or failure. With them rests people's happiness or misery." Mr. Toda, too, maintained that leaders are responsible for others' lives. That is why they must not be foolish, but, rather, study hard, make many times the effort of others, become truly capable people and pray earnestly for the happiness of their fellow members. This, emphasized Mr. Toda, must be the philosophy of leadership that guides the leaders of the Soka Gakkai.

Like One's Own Children

K'ung-ming also said:

All the great leaders of the past cared for the people as if they were their own children. In times of hardship, they leapt to action; when the glory was parceled out, they stepped back and encouraged others to come forward. They tenderly nursed the wounded, and solemnly buried and mourned those who fell in battle. They offered their own food to the hungry and their own clothing to the cold. They treated talented people with respect and gave them positions of responsibility, and they rewarded and honored the brave.

If leaders always behave in this fashion, they are certain to enjoy victory in every instance.

Such is the image of leadership described by K'ung-ming.

I hope you will all be leaders who share the sufferings and joys of your fellow members to whom you are linked by profound bonds. I hope you will always be thinking of their welfare, asking yourselves whether they are hungry or hot or cold or worried about something. Please share their joys and their sufferings. The sincerity of such caring leaders is what forges solid unity of purpose throughout the organization.

Starting the Day Early

Mr. Toda once said, "People in positions of leadership should make a point of going in to work early and, whether they have work to do or not, they should be sitting there [when everyone else arrives]."

And, in fact, Mr. Toda always got to work very early.

At that time, I was commuting from my home in Kobayashi-cho, in Ota Ward, to Mr. Toda's company in Ichigaya. I was not very strong physically, and Soka Gakkai activities stretched into the late hours of the night. Nevertheless, one fond memory of my youth is how I resolved and challenged myself to arrive at the office even before Mr. Toda and greet him fully prepared for the new day.

Be Strong of Heart!

Mr. Toda used to warn us, "The truer the teaching, the more numerous its opponents!"

The sutras speak of an "age of conflict." The Latter Day of the Law is a period of unceasing strife and contention.

Nichiren wrote, "If the general were to lose heart, his soldiers would become cowards" (WND-1, 613). Leaders need to be strong. Strength is the key to happiness; it also enables us to protect our members.

I hope you will all be resolute and strong of heart, demonstrating brilliant leadership like that of Chuko K'ung-ming, and achieve victory after victory.

The Power of Women Is Tremendous

Among the leaders gathered today are many from the women's division, whose members are cultivating an ever-expanding network of dialogue and friendship across the land. Thank you for all your hard work!

Mr. Toda used to say to the women's division members: "We'll be in a terrible fix if we can't accomplish *kosen-rufu* in the present age. Our success in achieving that goal will be determined by the efforts of women."

He valued the women's division very highly and sternly reprimanded any male leader who was arrogant, patronizing or authoritarian toward our devoted women's division members.

It is important for male leaders to address women with the utmost courtesy and respect, sincerely thanking them for their efforts and offering them warm words of encouragement.

Mr. Toda wholeheartedly praised the activities of the women's and young women's divisions, saying: "The power of women is tremendous. Also, in terms of their active contribution to the Soka Gakkai's growth and development, women are always one step ahead of men."

I, too, would like to express my supreme gratitude for the enormous strides being made by our women and young women, who are continuing to open new doors for *kosen-rufu* in the twenty-first century. I want to support them in every way I possibly can.

In closing, I offer my sincere prayers for your health and happiness.

Thank you.

From the August 4, 2003, Seikyo Shimbun

Notes

1 Aeschylus, *The Oresteia: Agamemnon, The Liberation Bearers, The Eumenides,* translated by Robert Fagles (New York: Quality Paperback Book Club, 1994), p. 274, l. 985.

2 Aeschylus, *Prometheus Bound,* in *Prometheus Bound, The Supplicants, Seven Against Thebes, The Persians,* translated by Philip Vellacott (London: Penguin Books, 1961), p. 53.

3 Cicero, *De Officiis,* in *Cicero in Twenty-eight Volumes,* translated by Walter Miller (London: William Heinemann Ltd., 1968), vol. 21, p. 51.

4 André Maurois, *The Art of Living,* translated by James Whitall (New York: Harper & Brothers Publishers, 1940), p. 227.

5 All quotes attributed to Chuko K'ung-ming in this speech are from the Japanese writer Eiji Yoshikawa's novel *Sangoku Shi* (Three Kingdoms).

Kosen-rufu Will Advance to the Same Degree That Leaders Grow

AUGUST 3, 2003

Let us talk together for the sake of *kosen-rufu.*

No new value can be created if we stay rigidly attached to how things have been done in the past. Leaders must constantly ask themselves: "How can we move forward? What can we do, so that everyone can advance with enthusiasm and fresh hope?"

One important key to achieving this, I believe, is for men to take greater initiative and set a shining example for everyone. The women's division is a crucial force in our organization, serving as the mainstay of our Gakkai activities. It is, therefore, vital that men, and in particular the men's division, likewise rise to action and devote themselves to *kosen-rufu* in earnest.

Each of us must start by challenging ourselves. It may seem like a simple thing, but if each of us does this, it will set in motion a momentous wave of change. Let us challenge ourselves anew now.

It is also important to clarify goals and responsibilities. These, too, of course, must not be forced on others. Also, people will not feel motivated to make a genuine effort if such things are conveyed to them in a mechanical or bureaucratic manner. We need to communicate our spirit. We need to touch others' hearts and inspire them.

As leaders, please put all of your wisdom and intellect to work on creating a rhythm of successive victories.

Be Strong in Spirit!

Tolstoy was fond of the writings of Henri-Frédéric Amiel, the nineteenth-century Swiss writer and philosopher. Amiel observed in his well-known journal, "The enervated are unfortunate."[1] If we lose our vitality and vigor, we will be defeated, and we mustn't let that happen. Associating with weak-spirited people can also lead to misfortune. The challenges of life test the strength of our spirit. Those who possess a vital, vigorous spirit triumph. That is life. Buddhism enables us to summon limitless vitality and vigor.

Amiel also wrote, "Doing good requires courage."[2] Courage is essential if you wish to do good, the philosopher tells us. President Toda used to say, "It can be hard to summon compassion, but courage can take the place of compassion." We have the invincible Mystic Law; let us advance with the greatest courage there is.

Repose Exists in Effort

Amiel further noted in his journal: "It is the struggle, the activity, that is the law. We can only find repose in effort."[3] He is right. This is a principle of Buddhism as well.

Buddhism is action. It is never-ending advancement. Though we may encounter buffeting waves, raging storms and even blizzards on our way, it is important that we press onward with grit and tenacity, striving to build an undefeatable self. By doing so, we put into practice the Buddhist teaching that "obstacles equal peace and comfort."

Nothing Is Impossible with Unity

Last October, I met with President John Agyekum Kufuor of Ghana during his visit to Japan, and we spoke about the century of Africa.

The father of Ghanaian independence and the nation's first president, Kwame Nkrumah, declared, "I know that if we work together in friendly cooperation, nothing is impossible."[4] This is very true.

Cooperation, solidarity, the unity of "many in body, one in mind" are indispensable. Nichiren Daishonin wrote, "People can definitely attain their goal, if they are of one mind" (WND-1, 618). This is the Buddhist formula for victory.

Not Advancing Is Regressing

Tolstoy declared, "If you are doing nothing, it means you are doing bad things."[5] This is a perfect description of those who have betrayed and turned against the Soka Gakkai, to which they owed so much. Laboring under the delusion of their own importance, they grew arrogant, looked down on sincere, dedicated members and were lax in their own daily practice. Such behavior itself marked them as people who were already defeated.

A life dedicated to *kosen-rufu* demands that we strengthen our faith "day by day and month after month" (WND-1, 997). Not advancing is regressing.

If you remain unfocused, your life will flash by in a moment. Don't worry about what others say or how you are criticized or attacked. As long as you continue to advance with the Soka Gakkai, the organization of faith directly connected to the Daishonin, you are certain to triumph in the end.

President Makiguchi said, "You cannot become a person of great good if you allow yourself to be influenced by the praise or blame of others."

It is vital that we all stand up as courageous lions and exert ourselves energetically for *kosen-rufu*. Together let us crown our lives with victory, like a wonderful drama or a beautiful dance.

Wisdom Arises From a Sense of Responsibility

Once, when discussing the organization for *kosen-rufu*, Mr. Makiguchi remarked: "Organizational concerns are the most fundamental issue facing any enterprise. The bigger the enterprise grows, the more carefully and stringently organizational matters must be carried out."

Wisdom arises from a sense of responsibility. A conference, for example, will be unsuccessful if members see it as just more of the same old thing. Maintaining freshness and creativity are important.

In terms of study as well, you will be lacking in compassion unless you make a special effort to help everyone understand Buddhist teachings fully. Study is an important tool for all our members, to help them win in life, advance *kosen-rufu* and defeat evil and injustice.

Faith is the only fundamental way to happiness. People who lose sight of that and lead empty lives end up in sad and tragic circumstances.

Let us raise our children in the garden of *kosen-rufu*.

Leaders Need To Grow

Leaders need to be constantly studying and improving themselves. When I was a youth, Mr. Toda trained me strictly, constantly urging me to study and read good books. This is my greatest treasure. *Kosen-rufu* will advance to the same degree that leaders grow. Please remember that.

To live a life dedicated to *kosen-rufu* is to live in a realm of supreme pride, benefit, responsibility and happiness. With hope and confidence, please build joyous and triumphant local organizations—great citadels of the Law—in the respective places of your mission.

From the August 5, 2003, Seikyo Shimbun

NOTES

1 Translated from the French. Henri-Frédéric Amiel, *Journal intime* (Private Journal) (Lausanne, Switzerland: L'Age d'Homme, 1991), vol. 10 (June 1874–March 1877), p. 795.

2 Translated from the French. Henri-Frédéric Amiel, *Fragments d'un journal intime* (Fragments of a Private Journal) (Geneva: Georg & Co Libraires-Éditeurs, 1911), vol. 1, p. 202.

3 Translated from the French. Henri-Frédéric Amiel, *Journal intime* (Private Journal) (Lausanne, Switzerland: L'Age d'Homme,1976), vol. 1 (1839–1851), p. 939.

4 Kwame Nkrumah, *I Speak of Freedom* (London: Panaf Books Limited, 1973), p. 37.

5 Leo Tolstoy, *A Calendar of Wisdom,* translated by Peter Sekirin (New York: Scribner, 1997), p. 250.

Unity Is the Starting Point for Victory

AUGUST 4, 2003

Chuko K'ung-ming [also known as Zhuge Liang] was an ancient Chinese hero whom second Soka Gakkai president Josei Toda admired tremendously. I recall with great fondness the days of my youth when I studied *The Romance of the Three Kingdoms,* in which K'ung-ming figures as a leading character.

In the third century, China was divided into three kingdoms: the powerful Wei in the north, ruled by Ts'ao Ts'ao; Wu in the southeast, ruled by Sun Ch'üan; and Shu Han in the southwest, ruled by Liu Pei, whom K'ung-ming served as a general and prime minister. Fierce power struggles and conflicts unfolded between the states. In this turbulent era, K'ung-ming, on whose shoulders the destiny of the Shu Han state rested, fought valiantly to preserve his homeland.

All of you gathered here today are the Chuko K'ung-mings of the Soka Gakkai.

I have spoken on this subject on several past occasions, but today I would like to talk about K'ung-ming's theories of leadership, his methods of fostering talented individuals and his approach to struggles.

Gathering Wisdom Around You

K'ung-ming said, "The foundation of good government is listening to the opinions of others."[1]

This was a core principle of his vision of leadership. When you are leading a large group, it is important to not just talk *at* them. You need to listen to others' opinions, draw out the issues of concern and pool everyone's wisdom. From there, a great wave of fresh advancement will spread out.

K'ung-ming created an assembly where he gathered representatives from throughout the kingdom, held conferences and listened to the representatives' opinions.

He was a leader who took initiative. Everyone is watching what those in leadership positions do, he said. A leader, therefore, must be a model for others.

Never Let an Opportunity Slip Away

Don't let important opportunities slip away—this was the guiding philosophy behind K'ung-ming's successive victories.

He said, "One should regret the loss of the smallest amount of time more than the loss of precious jewels, because opportunities are harder to come by and easier to lose." Once an opportunity is gone, it will never return; therefore, don't let it slip away, he says.

K'ung-ming also said, "To be ready to seize an opportunity when it arrives, a superior leader does not untie his belt to relax or walk so slowly that he leaves footprints." In other words, he is ready to grab an opportunity and make the most of it without delay.

Stay Alert

K'ung-ming was bold and daring in battle. He said: "Those on the front lines must not stand still," and "The soldiers in the vanguard must not rise and then stand motionless. If they do, they will obstruct the crossbows behind them."

Mr. Toda also used to warn leaders on the front lines not to be lackadaisical or unfocused. A step or two forward by our vanguard leaders will open the path ahead.

If leaders are not alert, they will get in the way of those following them. This represents failure as a leader.

Never Be Arrogant

What are the qualities required for leaders on whom a country's prosperity rests? K'ung-ming stated emphatically that leaders must not be arrogant.

He said: "If leaders are arrogant, they will become discourteous, and if they are discourteous, they will lose the support of others. If they lose the support of others, the people will rebel."

If leaders become high-handed and disrespectful, they will alienate people and lose their allegiance. This is a rule that applies to all nations and organizations.

K'ung-ming also warned leaders not to associate with people lacking in virtue, "Associate with wise ministers, but keep your distance from those without virtue."

This is the way to ensure that a nation will flourish.

Unsuitable As Leaders

K'ung-ming also cites eight kinds of people who are not suitable as leaders. They are people who:

1. Have unlimited greed for wealth
2. Are envious of people of talent and ability
3. Delight in maligning others and associating with flatterers
4. Are quick to analyze the faults of others but have no true understanding of themselves
5. Are hesitant and indecisive
6. Are overly fond of alcoholic beverages and can't control themselves
7. Are hypocritical and cowardly
8. Are smooth talkers with an arrogant, rude manner

Mr. Toda strictly warned leaders: "It doesn't matter what others do. Everything depends on you, on your determination."

Everything is decided by the leaders' inner resolve. As wise leaders, please engrave this point in your hearts.

Approach to Struggles

A battle once begun must be won. K'ung-ming was very strict in his advice to leaders embarking on a struggle. He was, in other words, strict with himself.

He said, "If even a single person is harmed, it is my personal responsibility."

K'ung-ming's philosophy of leadership was based on a highly developed awareness and sense of responsibility for the welfare of others. He was determined to prevent even a single individual from being harmed, left behind or made unhappy.

K'ung-ming also outlined four points that leaders engaged in a struggle should always remember:

1. Use new, unexpected strategies.
2. Plan thoroughly and carefully.
3. Act calmly and quietly.
4. Unite the hearts and minds of your forces.

Constant Vigilance

In K'ung-ming's famous declaration of loyalty to his ruler [Liu Ch'an, heir and successor to Liu Pei], he said, "I will bend my back to the task until my dying day."

This was a passage the great Chinese premier Zhou Enlai, the Chuko K'ung-ming of the twentieth century, often recited.

In his declaration, K'ung-ming also looked back on his past struggles, saying:

> From the day I was entrusted with my office under the former ruler [Liu Pei], I have never rested easy while I slept, never leisurely savored my food when I ate, but only sought to carry out my duty with utter dedication.

And articulating a leader's unshakable commitment, he wrote:

> Though honored, he will not be arrogant; though entrusted with power, he will not act arbitrarily; though rescued by another, he will not hide that dishonor; though relieved of his position, he will not show surprise or fear. Therefore, the actions of a superior leader are never agitated, no matter what the circumstances, just as a pure jewel can never be sullied.

Leaders who possess an invincible fighting spirit triumph. Please demonstrate wise leadership like K'ung-ming.

Forewarnings of Defeat

Every event has some foreshadowing that we can see if we are observant. This is especially true of defeat, which is always forewarned and has an identifiable cause.

K'ung-ming named several warning signs for an organization's imminent defeat:

1. The leaders become weak.

   This is a decisive factor in defeat. Leaders need to have a strong desire to triumph and be prepared to devote their very lives to encourage their fellow members. It is no exaggeration to say that victory and defeat depend entirely on the fighting spirit of our leaders.

2. People become self-serving and form cliques.

   When people are motivated by self-interest, they lose sight of the organization's goals.

3. People form factions and engage in intrigue against others in order to promote their own interests.

   Mr. Toda would not tolerate people who tried to form cliques or factions in the Soka Gakkai. He strictly reprimanded them and made sure they eliminated their arrogance.

4. People with twisted natures who flatter their superiors are placed in positions of power.

   When flatterers are placed in positions of responsibility, people become afraid of their power and reluctant to speak up.

All of these, K'ung-ming says, foreshadow defeat.

Characteristics of a Successful Organization

K'ung-ming also listed several requirements for a winning organization:

1. Talented individuals are given leadership roles.
2. The organization as a whole has high morale and unity.
3. There are good relations between leaders and members.
4. Everyone carefully follows instructions.
5. Everyone exerts himself or herself courageously and earnestly.
6. The organization overflows with an atmosphere of confidence and dignity.
7. Rewards and penalties are implemented fairly and impartially.

Unity is of vital importance for the Soka Gakkai, as are high spirits. Let us advance courageously, earnestly and confidently.

Fostering Capable People for Victory

How do we foster and make the best use of capable people who will ensure victory? K'ung-ming valued not only ability but character. He was not concerned with a person's social status or position.

"My heart is impartial. I do not judge people based on personal prejudice." This was K'ung-ming's creed.

And with regard to selecting talented people, K'ung-ming said:

> When superior leaders govern, they allow others to choose talented people instead of making all the appointments themselves. People's accomplishments should be

measured by objective standards, not by arbitrary inclination or personal prejudice. If that system is adopted, talented people will not be overlooked and incapable people will not be placed in positions of power.

K'ung-ming also warned: "The greatest contribution one can make in the name of loyalty is to recommend talented people. But when recommending others, people tend to be swayed by their own preferences."

We must absolutely not permit a situation to arise where leaders, guided by personal prejudice, cause countless others to suffer. It is important to praise and sincerely support those who are striving the hardest. I hope you will all become the kind of selfless leader who does just that.

K'ung-ming also said: "Not everyone is keen-witted. Not all horses are champions. Not all tools are sturdily made. Because of that, we have to make optimum use of what we have."

Nothing in our world is perfect. We must make the best of each individual's good points, he says.

The Strength and Courage To Deal with Any Contingency

K'ung-ming offered the following seven methods for appraising a person's character:

1. Observe whether the person's resolve or attitude changes in response to rumors or the opinions of others.
2. See how the person responds when subjected to a stern rebuke.
   A person's true character tends to reveal itself when he or she is harshly taken to task.

3. Inquire about the person's plans and opinions to measure his or her knowledge and judgment.

   This will also indicate the person's sense of responsibility.

4. Proclaim there is an emergency and observe the person's courage and strength in dealing with it.

   Courage and strength in an emergency are certainly indispensable qualities for leaders.

5. Observe how the person behaves when drinking alcohol.

6. Test the person's integrity by offering benefits and privileges.

7. Assign the person an important task and observe his or her trustworthiness.

Undesirable Elements

K'ung-ming further urged that we should keep our distance from the following five kinds of people, because they are likely to cause trouble, whether in a state or an organization. I would like to present them here as a warning for the future:

1. People who form cliques and factions and are envious of and slander those of upstanding character.

2. Vain people who are overly fond of fancy clothes and seek to attract attention.

3. People who sow confusion through exaggeration and misrepresentation.

4. People who try to manipulate others out of self-interest or desire for personal gain.

5. People who care only for their own advantage and forge secret alliances with enemies.

Remaining Faithful to Our Beliefs

What is the most quintessential quality that defines us as human beings? According to K'ung-ming, it is to remain faithful to our beliefs. He said:

> The spirit of fidelity in a human being is like a fish being in deep water. Just as a fish will die if its water disappears, if people lose faith in their convictions, they will cause harm to society and other people. That is why a good leader is faithful. In this way, his aspirations will be achieved and he will gain a fine reputation.

Have High Aspirations

K'ung-ming urged future generations to have high aspirations and not to lead empty, meaningless lives. He said:

> If your will is not strong and invincible, if you are bereft of passion, you will idle away your life without attempting anything of note, imprisoned by feelings of emptiness, forever trapped in the ordinary, never escaping from the lowliest level of existence.

If you avoid all effort and seek only ease and comfort, your spirit will wither and stagnate. Don't live an empty, meaningless life! Dedicate your life to the highest good, to realizing your mission, to carrying out the responsibility entrusted to you! This is our faith. By taking on this challenge, we can lead lives of boundless hope, fulfillment and value-creation.

K'ung-ming warned his own child:

A wise person purifies his heart and disciplines his body, making a sincere effort to cultivate virtue. Unless you are free of attachments and personal desires, your aspirations will never be clear, and unless you are quiet and calm, your thoughts will never range far.

We are the product of our aspirations. By pursuing our aspirations and ideals throughout our lives, we can lead genuinely great lives.

True Friendship

Let me close today by sharing K'ung-ming's words about true friendship with you:

It is difficult to long sustain opportunistic relationships. The acquaintance of true friends does not add flowers in warm times or change its leaves in cold times; it never fades throughout the four seasons, only growing stronger as it weathers good times and bad.

Let us reach out and forge many precious new friendships throughout this summer.

From the August 6, 2003, Seikyo Shimbun

NOTES

1 The quotes attributed to K'ung-ming in this essay are all translated from Japanese sources.

Wielding the Power of Speech in Defense of Justice

AUGUST 4, 2003

The words of the wise cast an eternal illumination. For example, this saying attributed to the ancient Roman philosopher Marcus Tullius Cicero has been a precious source of inspiration for me since my youth, "A room without books is like a body without a soul."

Cicero, who is hailed as the father of his country, was also a brilliant statesman, lawyer and orator renowned for his eloquent speech.

Speaking of eloquence, Tokyo Soka Senior High School's debating team has taken the top prize in the National Junior and Senior High School Debating Championships for the third time and for the second consecutive year. The Tokyo Soka Junior High School debating team also placed third in their division. As the school's founder, this makes me very happy.

During an age of turmoil, Cicero used speech and philosophy to fight against corrupt and evil authorities and to assist the persecuted and oppressed. Many of his superb speeches have been handed down to us today.

Cicero was also a prolific author, writing on many subjects with great power. Among his surviving works are *On the Republic, On*

Duties and *On Ends*. His essays were regarded as a model of perfection in Europe and had a profound influence on the development of European culture.

Be Champions of Speech

Offering words of hope in an age of turmoil is also the Soka Gakkai tradition. I ask that all of you strive to become brilliant and inspiring orators, the kind of speakers about whom others say enthusiastically: "I really look forward to hearing her speak again," or "He really made that discussion meeting unforgettable!"

What matters is not superficial appearances but sincerity and personal courage. Even the briefest remark—a thank-you or an inquiry about someone's family—can be an immense source of encouragement and have a tremendous ripple effect.

Please be champions of speech who are renowned for their deeply moving personal warmth, for their powerful conviction that jolts others to question misguided views and achieve a new level of awareness and for their persuasive logic that clarifies the truth and refutes error and injustice.

Cherishing Lofty Aspirations

Society is rife with envy and ego and intrigue. Before setting sail into a society that is as perilous as a stormy sea, young people must make a genuine effort to advance toward a lofty goal. Cicero proclaimed that youth "ought to set their sights on great things and strive for them with unswerving devotion."[1] I remember that my mentor, second Soka Gakkai president Josei Toda, often used to say, "Young people should cherish dreams that seem almost too big to accomplish."

When Cicero was a young man, he witnessed a fellow citizen plunged into the most abject circumstances as a result of being falsely accused of wrongdoing through the machinations of villains. This incident was the catalyst that spurred Cicero to hone his ability to speak out for truth and justice.

Later, Cicero pleaded the case of another person who stood unjustly accused, and in doing so he publicly attacked the dictatorial authorities. He had obtained the confidence that, with words as his weapon, he could triumph over the forces of evil and corruption.

Cicero lamented, "Now it is a sort of blot and blemish of this age to be envious of virtue, to seek to crush merit in its very bloom."[2] Those who ascend to the summit of a towering peak are buffeted by fierce winds. Persecution assails greatness.

Nevertheless, malicious attacks must not go unchallenged. "The purpose of this [setting forth our case]," said Cicero, "was not that we might by what was said prove to you what was so obvious, but that we might overcome the hostility of all those who are malevolent, unjust, and envious."[3]

Throughout his life, Cicero was committed to achieving justice through his oratory. He declared:

Let me . . . denounce the insolence of the villains.[4]

* * *

Justice must be cultivated and maintained by every method.[5]

* * *

The man who does not defend someone, or obstruct the injustice when he can, is at fault just as if he had abandoned his parents or his friends or his country.[6]

Cicero stressed the necessity of resolutely speaking out against evil and corruption.

Those who don't defend the truth or resist what is wrong end up allowing others to suffer. Although they may give the impression of being nice, affable people, they are in fact very foolish. It is crucial that we speak out against each injustice and correct each falsehood.

Friends Are a Source of Strength

Many were envious of Cicero's fame and upstanding reputation, but he also had true friends. Cicero often spoke about friendship. He said:

> Seeing that friendship includes very many and very great advantages, it undoubtedly excels all other things in this respect, that it projects the bright ray of hope into the future, and does not suffer the spirit to grow faint or to fall.[7]
>
> * * *
>
> The real friend . . . is, as it were, another self.[8]

Friends in whom we can trust, who share the same ideals and goals, are a source of strength, a source of hope and enrich our lives.

"My Ability Is All Due to My Mentor"

One of Cicero's most famous orations, a mighty lion's roar of truth, was his defense of his mentor, the poet Aulus Licinius Archias. This man, under whom Cicero studied literature as a youth, had been falsely accused of a crime and was in danger of being banished from Rome. Needless to say, the charges against him were nothing but an insidious plot concocted by the authorities. When Cicero rose up to defend his teacher in court, he boldly declared:

> If there be any natural ability in me, O judges, . . . this Aulus Licinius is entitled to be among the first to claim the benefit from me as his peculiar right. . . . Undoubtedly we ought, as far as lies in our power, to help and save the very man from whom we have received that gift.[9]

In his speech Cicero referred to his mentor as "a most sublime poet,"[10] and largely due to Cicero's defense, the name of Aulus Licinius Archias has been recorded for all posterity.

The Destiny of Nations and Organizations Depends on Their Leaders

I have visited the ruins of ancient Rome and seen the Roman Forum where Cicero spoke. [*In October 1961, when SGI President Ikeda was 33.*] I composed the following poem at that time:

> Standing here
> Amid the ruins of ancient Rome,
> I think:
> The kingdom of the Mystic Law
> Will never perish.

When a nation or organization is defeated and declines, the reasons are always complex; leaders, however, are a major factor. For instance, leaders who don't know the first thing about hard work; leaders who can't appreciate others' feelings; leaders who always take the easiest course requiring the least amount of effort; leaders who have a high opinion of themselves but in fact achieve nothing of substance; leaders who don't support or encourage those who are genuinely working hard and making tremendous contributions; leaders who are ignorant of people's personal circumstances and situations; leaders who give responsible positions to irresponsible, unreliable individuals—such leaders are a cause of failure.

President Toda dealt with such leaders in the sternest fashion.

It is vital for our leaders to chant wholeheartedly, exert every possible effort and open the way forward with every ounce of their being, so that everyone can savor the joy of victory and advance courageously and vibrantly.

The struggle to win is demanding. It is a challenge. It all comes down to whether leaders have the earnest desire to win that struggle. Tenacity and perseverance are the key. I would particularly like our youth division leaders to engrave this in their lives in the midst of their endeavors for *kosen-rufu*.

SGI-Italy: Creating a Beautiful Network of Friendship and Trust

Right now, SGI-Italy, which is continuing its dynamic growth, is making great and joyous strides for peace and culture. Its members are building a beautiful network of friendship and trust in society. In support of their humanistic activities, a province has named a street and two cities have named parks after our first president, Tsunesaburo Makiguchi. Nothing could make me happier. I also fondly recall the commemorative lecture I was invited to give at the venerable University of Bologna, one of the world's oldest universities.

[Italy's Perugia Province has named a street after Tsunesaburo Maki-guchi; the city of Capraia e Limite in Florence Province has designated a Tsunesaburo Makiguchi Peace Park; and the city of Stia in Arezzo Province has dedicated a Plaza of Peace to the Soka Gakkai's founding president. SGI President Ikeda received an honorary doctorate from the University of Bologna in June 1994. In addition, he is the recipient of honorary citizenship awards from 41 Italian cities.]

Cicero called out to the leaders of Rome, "[No power can] be found which will be able to undermine and destroy your union with the Roman knights, and such unanimity as exists among all good men."[11]

Cicero's name stands as one of the towering summits of history. Let us also create a proud achievement that will shine forever in the eternal history of *kosen-rufu*.

The Purpose of the Soka Gakkai Is Kosen-rufu and World Peace

The objective of many enterprises is to increase their wealth. The goal of nations is to prosper and develop.

What then is the purpose of the Soka Gakkai? It is *kosen-rufu* and world peace. It is increasing the number of Bodhisattvas of the Earth. This is the task that Nichiren has entrusted to us.

That is why those who work for *kosen-rufu* are noble beyond measure. The foundation of working for *kosen-rufu* is the spirit of *shakubuku*. It is the desire to help another friend, to create one more ally. This is the most important thing of all and results in infinite benefit. It is also the underlying strength of the Soka Gakkai.

The world is waiting for humanism. Increasing our friends is a source of immense joy. Let us reach out to many new friends and together walk the great path toward happiness.

Let us wisely and joyously strengthen our wonderful alliance of Soka as we chant in earnest and warmly encourage and support one another.

From the August 7, 2003, Seikyo Shimbun

NOTES

1 Cicero, *On Duties,* in *Cambridge Texts in the History of Political Thought,* edited by M. T. Griffin and E. M. Atkins (Cambridge, UK: Cambridge University Press, 1991), Book II, pp. 79–80, section 45.

2 Cicero, "Pro Balbo," *Pro Caelio, De Provinciis Consularibus, Pro Balbo,* translated by R. Gardner (Cambridge, MA, and London: Harvard University Press & William Heinemann Ltd., 1970), vol. 13, p. 643, VI, 15.

3 Ibid., pp. 703–05, XXV, 56.

4 Cicero, *Cicero's Letters to Atticus,* translated by D. R. Shackleton Bailey (Middlesex, UK: Penguin Books, 1978), p. 386. Letter to Atticus, dated April 4, 49 BCE (X. Ia.).

5 Cicero, *On Duties,* Book II, p. 79, section 42.

6 Cicero, *On Duties,* Book I, p. 10, section 23.

7 Cicero, *De Senectute, De Amicitia, De Divinatione,* translated by William Armistead Falconer (London and Cambridge, MA: William Heinemann Ltd. & Harvard University Press, 1974), p. 133, VII, 23.

8 Ibid., p. 189, XXI, 80.

9 Cicero, *The Orations of Marcus Tullius Cicero,* translated by C. D. Yonge (London: Bell & Daldy, 1869), vol. 2, pp. 411–12. "The speech of M. T. Cicero for Aulus Licinius Archias, the Poet," section 1.

10 Ibid., p. 412, section 2.

11 Ibid., p. 328. "Against Catiline," fourth speech, section X.

You Are the Protagonist of Your Life

AUGUST 5, 2003

Thank you for your participation in these daily conference sessions for the sake of *kosen-rufu*. These meetings are very important, so I would like to speak to you again a bit today. I want to transmit to you a record of all the training and guidance I received from my mentor, second Soka Gakkai president Josei Toda. I want to help everyone establish a rhythm of victory in his or her life.

Let me start by sharing the words of several internationally renowned women.

A Life of Personal Victory

Helen Keller, who, though blind and deaf, became a famous social activist, wrote, "Our worst foes are not belligerent circumstances, but wavering spirits."[1] In other words, our greatest enemy is not adversity; our circumstances, whether good or bad, do not control our lives. We do. We are the protagonists of the drama of our lives. Keller also said, "It is not environment that alters a human being, but forces within him."[2] This is very similar to our philosophy of human revolution.

Above all, the most important thing is whether we find personal fulfillment in our lives. Victors in life are those who can declare, irrespective of what anyone else may say, "I did my best, and I won!"

Keller further wrote, "[Our] more enduring joys are born of an unselfish purpose to serve others and create new life in the world."³ We are working for the good of society, to bring hope and inspiration to others and to accomplish our personal missions in life. We are certain, therefore, to lead lives of joy and fulfillment.

Meeting and Talking With Others

In my dialogue with Dr. Hazel Henderson, the American futurist, we talked about the pioneering American environmental activist Rachel Carson. Remarking on her dreams while still a young woman, Carson said:

> Sometimes I lose sight of my goal, then again it flashes into view, filling me with a new determination to keep the "vision splendid" before my eyes. I may never come to a full realization of my dreams, but [as the English poet Robert Browning said] "a man's reach must exceed his grasp or what's a heaven for?"⁴

It is important to have high ideals and make a noble effort to realize them.

Let us set forth each day with eager resolve—"I'll do my best again today!" "I'll go and see this person!" "I'll talk with that person!"—brimming with a vibrant, positive youthful spirit, no matter what our age. That is the way of life of those who practice the Buddhism of true cause—the spirit of always starting fresh from this moment on.

People who are working hard for *kosen-rufu* always have a

sparkle. They are vitally alive. In fact, one of our guests praised the "radiance" of our women's division members. Practicing Nichiren Buddhism polishes our lives so that they shine with unsurpassed beauty and refinement.

Our Efforts Expand and Elevate Our State of Being

I'm sure you've all heard of Eleanor Roosevelt, wife of U.S. President Franklin Delano Roosevelt. The renowned economist John Kenneth Galbraith, with whom I am currently engaged in an ongoing dialogue, incidentally, enjoyed a friendship with the former American first lady.

Mrs. Roosevelt, while serving as an indispensable support for her husband after polio suddenly left him confined to a wheelchair, was a tireless campaigner for world peace and human rights. She wrote, "It is only an approximation [of the dream of perfection] that anyone can reach, but the closer one tries to approximate it, the more he will grow."[5]

Many of our women's division members in particular are engaging in activities for *kosen-rufu* while being a support to their husbands, raising their children and keeping their families together. Each step in those noble efforts infinitely expands and elevates their state of being.

The Victory of Prayer

The French writer Madame de Staël rebuked the authoritarian powers of her day. In her eloquent writings, she sharply exposed the evils dwelling within society and individuals.

Madame de Staël declared that conceit and disgrace are evils that result from vanity.[6] She also said, "Calculation is the laborer of genius, the servant of the soul; but if it becomes the master, there is no longer anything grand or noble in man."[7] These words are certainly an apt description of the pitifully declining Nichiren Shoshu priesthood. As you are well aware, not only the former high priest Nikken and his cohorts but all malicious people who have persecuted the Soka Gakkai in its dedication to truth and justice have traveled a path leading to decline and ruin.

In contrast, the Soka Gakkai has won over all, affirming the Daishonin's statement, "Buddhism primarily concerns itself with victory or defeat" (WND-1, 835). This victory has been due largely to the unceasing efforts of our women's division and young women's division members, who have struggled earnestly for *kosenrufu*, come rain or shine. Indeed, the Soka Gakkai has triumphed through your strong faith and tenacious prayers.

Madame de Staël also said, "It belongs alone to philosophy, founded upon religion, to inspire an unalterable resolution under all contingencies."[8] I sincerely praise and express my deepest appreciation for the valiant efforts to advance our movement being made by the women's division and young women's division members.

One Autumn Day at the Soka Schools

Raisa Gorbachev, the late wife of former Soviet president Mikhail Gorbachev, is someone my wife and I will never forget. We were most fortunate to share several meaningful encounters with her. She died in 1999, but her wise, smiling countenance remains alive in my heart to this day.

In November 1997, we invited Mr. and Mrs. Gorbachev to visit the Soka Schools in Kansai. They were very happy at the warm welcome the students gave them, and they often spoke fondly of the occasion afterward. That day at the height of autumn, surrounded by the brightness of youth, was our last meeting with Raisa Gorbachev.

Mrs. Gorbachev expressed a deep understanding of and sympathy with our movement. She once said: "I felt again the greatness of the Soka Gakkai. The members are all such wonderful people, so full of life and vigor, and they have such pride in their movement."

At one time, when she was being driven around Kyoto by one of our event staff, Mrs. Gorbachev learned that he was the president of a large company and had volunteered his time to serve as a driver. She said to him with gratitude: "It is wonderful to see a person contributing to society as an individual human being, regardless of social position or importance. Russia has much to learn from this spirit."

"As an individual human being"—Mrs. Gorbachev's thoughts always started and ended with that focus. When Russia was undergoing dramatic changes, some succumbed to the easy temptations of hatred and destruction, but the Soviet Union's former first lady, pained by those developments, spoke out as one human being: "Is destruction necessary for progress? That goes against common sense. I am convinced that only that which is constructive can make people happy."

Mrs. Gorbachev worked very hard to bring about the dawn of an age in which women can realize their full potential as individuals. At one conference, she said: "Women and peace are inseparable. By their very nature, women bring peace and cooperation to society."

The Struggle To Leave a Record of the Truth

Both Mr. and Mrs. Gorbachev gave their all to advancing the social, economic and political reforms of perestroika, but some tried to erase that important fact from history. The Gorbachevs responded by establishing the Perestroika Library and Archives, dedicated to preserving the truth for future generations.

Mrs. Gorbachev spoke of her thoughts on this at the Kansai Soka Schools: "In the past I used to think that reality and history were firm, unchanging things that could not be rebutted. Now I know, however, that historians only look at the aspects of history that they choose to, and even simple facts can be twisted out of shape. That is why it is so important to leave a written record to convey what really happened."

Conveying the truth entails a struggle. Without striving to ensure that facts are correctly recorded, the real history of events will be blurred and distorted—and that would be the greatest of misfortunes.

The same can be said of our struggle for *kosen-rufu*. If we fail, the path to happiness and peace for the human race will be closed forever. That is why we must not lose.

Indeed, in any challenge we take on for *kosen-rufu*, it is important for us to emerge victorious.

I strongly urge you, for the sake of humanity's future, to speak out indefatigably and powerfully for truth and justice.

Fostering Capable People

Soong Ching-ling [Song Qingling], the wife of Sun Yat-sen, father of the Chinese Revolution, was also a champion of reform. She insisted:

> The education of the next generation is the responsibility of the nation as a whole. . . . To foster those of the next generation as successors to our great enterprise, . . . our

legacy to them must not only be of a material nature but, far more important, we must pass on to them our revolutionary spirit.[9]

The noblest and most challenging task is how to nurture successors for *kosen-rufu* in our families and communities. And the vital factor here is, as Madame Soong states, the sense of responsibility of those involved in this undertaking.

A sense of responsibility is manifested in prayer and action, which in turn further deepen our sense of responsibility. It is also crucial to chant earnestly for capable people to appear and for them to grow and develop so that they can make great contributions. Everything opens up from there.

Madame Soong had a message for young people, too: "You must go and learn among the people. . . . You must advance with the people."[10] Why? Youth is the period in life when we ask the fundamental questions, such as "Who am I?" and "How should I live my life?" She is saying that the answers to those questions are to be found among the people, in advancing in step with the people.

Madame Soong also called out to the women of Asia: "The undeniable reality before us is the ultimate victory of the people. . . . Let us take courage! With even greater vigilance and effort, let us fight!"[11]

Ending Meetings on Time

We are living in a troubled age with violent crime soaring even here in Japan. I would like you all to remain safe and secure and to attain happiness. That is my sincerest prayer.

As I have said many times, please ensure that meetings end on time, and don't allow discussions after meetings to continue to a late hour. I would like the young women's division members in particular to observe these guidelines stringently, even if it means erring on the side of caution. I especially ask our young women not to walk alone at night; it's safer to walk together in groups of two or three. If for any reason you are going to be home later than expected, please call your family and let them know. I hope leaders will do their utmost to ensure our members' safety and security. Genuine leaders in faith pay attention to such details.

Give a Smile!

Nichiren wrote to his youthful disciple Nanjo Tokimitsu about the importance of treating his parents with kindness and respect and outlined four virtues taught by Chinese sages of times past:

> First, being filial toward one's father and mother means that though a parent may act unreasonably or speak in a tone of ill will, one never shows the slightest anger or looks displeased. (WND-2, 636)

Though your parents may always seem to be scolding you, try not to react in a negative way. Instead, attempt to listen to the feelings behind their words. That effort on your part is often enough to put their minds at ease. All parents worry about their children. Of course, everyone's circumstances are different, but the important thing is to keep the lines of communication open.

The Daishonin went on to say:

> One never in any way disobeys a parent; is always mindful of providing a parent with all manner of good things, and if this happens to be impossible, in the course of a day

one at least smiles twice or thrice in their direction. (WND-2, 636)

This is really touching guidance. Smile and ask your father how he's feeling, or thank your mother for her hard work. That alone can be enough to bring tears of happiness to a parent's eye. The most important thing is to be considerate of others. That is compassion, and from that compassion will arise limitless wisdom and hope. This applies not only on the family level. Consideration for others is also the foundation for building trust at the community level and, on an even broader scale, among nations.

Our movement for *kosen-rufu* is nothing other than the effort to expand this fundamental Buddhist spirit of compassion throughout our community, our society and the world.

From the August 13, 2003, Seikyo Shimbun

NOTES

1 Joseph P. Lash, *Helen and Teacher: The Story of Helen Keller and Anne Sullivan Macy* (New York: Delacorte Press, 1980), p. 310.
2 Helen Keller, *My Religion* (New York: Swedenborg Foundation, Inc., 1953), p. 163.
3 Ibid., p. 173.
4 Linda Lear, *Rachel Carson: Witness for Nature* (New York: Henry Holt and Company, 1997), p. 32.
5 Eleanor Roosevelt, *You Learn by Living* (New York: Harper and Brothers Publishers, 1960), p. 166.
6 Baroness Staël Holstein, *Germany* (London: John Murray, 1813), vol. 3, pp. 391–92.
7 Ibid., p. 180.
8 Ibid., p. 170.
9 Translated from Japanese. Soong Ching-ling, *So Keirei senshu* (Selected Writings of Soong Ching-ling), translated from Chinese by Fumiko Niki (Tokyo: Domesu Shuppan, 1979), p. 458.
10 Ibid., p. 238.
11 Ibid., pp. 277–78.

Courage Is the Key To Winning in Life

AUGUST 5, 2003

The realm of the Mystic Law embraces the entire cosmos. It is a realm that befriends all people, teaches a philosophy of peace and happiness and seeks to inspire a sense of joy. Leaders in this realm exist to bring happiness to others. Leaders of firm and solid faith will not allow their own petty, personal feelings to cause distress to others.

It is important that we cast aside all personal vanity and false pride. We must strive to attain an expansive and fearless inner state of being. The Soka Gakkai is a citadel of highly qualified experts in faith; it is a school for genuine practitioners of philosophy.

In front of the Gohonzon, no one is better than anyone else. We are all equally noble. Authorities often look down on the people, calling them a mindless flock of sheep. The Soka Gakkai, however, respects the people; we are a proud assembly of awakened, thinking people dedicated to *kosen-rufu*. All of us have a mission. Let us advance, our hearts united as one.

The more we involve ourselves in Gakkai activities, the more we stand to gain. We can accumulate immense benefit, help our friends break free from suffering and carry out our human revolution. While praying earnestly and taking time to individually encourage others, let us each write a brilliant personal history of achievement—wisely, enjoyably and victoriously.

Tolstoy once cited a quote by the American thinker Ralph Waldo Emerson, whose writings I greatly admire. In this quote, Emerson urges us to hold our heads high, telling us that our lives are not ornaments but have been given to us to be used. He further stresses that it is important to speak the truth and give serious thought to our duty as human beings rather than what other people think of us.[1]

Don't worry about what others think. Be yourself. Lift up your head, stand up tall and proudly carry out your mission.

"We Youth"

In life, every day is a new departure. The other day, I encouraged a person who was retiring, telling him, "Though you are retiring, always stay involved."

Let us warmly remind one another that we are comrades in the struggle for *kosen-rufu* for as long as we live—in fact, for all eternity—and continue to strive earnestly together. Even as we advance in years, let's always maintain a youthful spirit and create a rhythm in our lives that will enable us to keep working for *kosen-rufu*. There is no retirement age in life or in faith. An energetic spirit to work for *kosen-rufu* is proof of one's youthfulness. Even when first Soka Gakkai president Tsunesaburo Makiguchi was over seventy, he used the phrase, when speaking to his disciples, "we youth."

The workings of the human mind are extraordinarily subtle. Say, for example, your children grow up and you gain a degree of financial stability. As a result, you succumb to the mind-set that you can now rest on your laurels and get by with minimum effort. If you let that happen, however, you will not be able to make the closing chapter of your life a glorious one. You can be old at fifty if you've lost your fighting spirit. At the same time, there are "youths" of eighty still exerting themselves with burning enthusiasm. There is no reason to retire or hold back in the struggle for *kosen-rufu*. I hope you will all continue to advance vigorously and freely with your fellow members throughout your lives.

In the past, I delivered an invitational address at the Institut de France in Paris [in June 1989]. The French poet Jean de La Fontaine was a renowned member of this prestigious academic institution. In his famous work *Fables,* he wrote, "From time immemorial, the little people have suffered from the stupidities of the big and powerful."[2] The foolish acts of the authorities are the root of all evils. How great is the suffering they have wrought on the people! The twenty-first century is the age in which we must correct this perversion.

La Fontaine further warned to the effect, "Those who set a trap for others set a trap for themselves."[3] He also asserted, "Ingrates all finally die miserable."[4] Envious and ungrateful people destroy their own lives.

The final stage of life is very important. It is crucial that we hold fast to the path we have chosen to the end. I call upon you to bravely lead the way to victory, aiming first toward 2005 [the year marking the seventy-fifth anniversary of the Soka Gakkai's founding and the thirtieth anniversary of the SGI].

Standing Resolute in the Face of Persecution

From his exile on Sado Island, Nichiren wrote to his disciples with severity:

There are also those who appeared to believe in me, but began doubting when they saw me persecuted. They not only have forsaken the Lotus Sutra, but also actually think themselves wise enough to instruct me. The pitiful thing is that these perverse people must suffer in the Avichi hell even longer than the Nembutsu believers. (WND-1, 306)

President Toda often spoke about what happened when Mr. Makiguchi was imprisoned during World War II. Top leaders who had worked closely at the founding president's side abandoned their faith. Some of them even left the organization angrily cursing their mentor, to whom they owed so much. These were individuals who had previously acted as if they were Mr. Makiguchi's number-one disciples but, the moment they were faced with persecution, they denounced him. They repaid their mentor with betrayal. A person who would do this is the worst kind of enemy. Mr. Toda cried out that he was determined to avenge Mr. Makiguchi.

A number of top leaders also abandoned their faith after being imprisoned [as a result of the authorities' crackdown on the Gakkai during World War II]. When the wife of one of these leaders visited her husband in jail, she showed him a message she had written on the palm of her hand, "Give up your faith and get out of prison quickly." As a result, the man renounced his faith. Whenever that story came up after the war, Mr. Toda would explode with rage: "How dare such a person call himself a Gakkai member? How could he betray Mr. Makiguchi like that?" I will never forget Mr. Toda's deep and bitter anger.

Nichiren wrote, "If they were people who understood their obligations or were capable of reason, then out of two blows that fall on me, they would receive one in my stead" (WND-1, 828).

How wretched are the final years of those who act contrary to this spirit and betray their mentor, the Soka Gakkai and their own beliefs? We have all seen what a pitiful end such people come to.

"Great persecution and obstacles are inevitable on the road to *kosen-rufu*. Be firmly determined to overcome them!" This was the spirit with which President Toda thoroughly trained me. He entrusted the future to the youth division.

Nichiren noted:

> Many people have taken faith in this teaching. But because great persecutions, both official and otherwise, have repeatedly befallen me, though they followed me for a year or two, all of them later either abandoned their faith or turned against the Lotus Sutra. Or if they have not given way in their practice, they have done so in their heart. Or if they have not given way in their heart, they have done so in their practice. (WND-1, 941)

With these words, he is praising his model disciples, implying that, in contrast to such people, they have not abandoned their faith or practice and have shown splendid proof of their victory because of their profound faith.

If the root of faith is deep, then luxuriant branches of success and fulfillment in life will appear.

Obstacles Are a Source of Growth

Because we have opponents, we can grow. They make us stronger. Triumphing over momentous obstacles is how we become Buddhas. The Daishonin stated: "Devadatta was the foremost good friend to the Thus Come One Shakyamuni. In this age as well, it is not one's allies but one's powerful enemies who assist one's progress" (WND-1, 770).

And in the midst of harsh persecution, Nichiren wrote, "It seems to me that on the path to attain Buddhahood it may invariably be when one has done something like lay down one's life that one becomes a Buddha" (WND-1, 202). Those who devote themselves selflessly to propagating the teachings are true votaries of the Lotus Sutra.

Nichiren Daishonin declared: "I, Nichiren, am the foremost votary of the Lotus Sutra in the entire land of Jambudvipa. Therefore, people who ally themselves with those who slander me or treat me with malice deserve to meet with the greatest difficulties in Jambudvipa" (WND-1, 552). These words resound with the indomitable conviction of the Buddha of the Latter Day of the Law.

The Daishonin further stated:

> Although I, Nichiren, am not a man of wisdom, the devil king of the sixth heaven has attempted to take possession of my body. But I have for some time been taking such great care that he now no longer comes near me. Therefore, because the power of the heavenly devil is ineffectual against me, he instead possesses the ruler and his high officials, or foolish priests such as Ryokan, and causes them to hate me. (WND-1, 310)

He also wrote, "Once you become a disciple or lay supporter of the votary who practices the true Lotus Sutra in accord with the Buddha's teachings, you are bound to face the three types of enemies" (WND-1, 391).

To be persecuted for upholding what is right and true is the greatest of honors. Nothing significant can be achieved with halfhearted resolve or only half-serious commitment. A person of genuine faith advances resolutely in the face of hatred, insult and persecution.

Encountering obstacles is an honor; encountering obstacles is peace and comfort—this is the lion's roar of the Daishonin.

I learned the true essence of Nichiren Buddhism under my peerless mentor, Mr. Toda, who inherited this spirit of the Daishonin. It was through that training that I gained the ability to quickly perceive people's true nature.

Those who are genuinely striving with all their might to realize *kosen-rufu* I wish to praise most highly and protect forever.

Nichiren wrote, "Though various grave persecutions fall on me like rain and boil up like clouds, since they are for the sake of the Lotus Sutra, even these sufferings do not seem like sufferings at all" (WND-1, 191). He also stated:

> In the Lotus Sutra the Buddha states that some two thousand, two hundred and more years after his passing, in the last five-hundred-year period, when efforts are made to propagate this sutra throughout the land of Jambudvipa, the heavenly devil will take possession of people and attempt to prevent the dissemination of the sutra. It will happen then that those who have faith in the sutra will be cursed and attacked, driven from one place to another, and perhaps even killed. At that time, those who stand in the vanguard will win benefit as great as though they had given offerings to the Buddhas of the three existences and the ten directions. (WND-2, 775)

Kosen-rufu is the eternal path to world peace. The benefit that results from taking the lead on that path is infinite and boundless.

Winning With Courage and the Power of Prayer

Courage—this is the key to winning in life! Princess Marthe Bibesco, author of a biography of former British prime minister Winston Churchill, wrote, "It is impossible to have enough courage; we all need it, every sort, kind and variety of courage, according to our characters and circumstances; we need courage every day of our lives."[5] Courage gives us the strength to overcome trying and painful times.

Nichiren declared: "Life flashes by in but a moment. No matter how many terrible enemies you may encounter, banish all fears and never think of backsliding" (WND-1, 395).

Life is either win or lose. More important than a hundred intellectual theories is that we actually win. The history of the Soka Gakkai shines brilliantly with countless examples of people challenging obstacles with earnest prayer and triumphing over them.

Prayer is our most powerful "weapon." If we chant Nam-myoho-renge-kyo with all our hearts and continue to make efforts to challenge our situation, we will definitely win in the end. Our goal is that single word: *victory*.

Madame Soong Ching-ling [also Song Qingling; wife of Sun Yat-sen, the father of modern China] said, "Our unrivaled source of power is the unity of all the forces of the nation."[6] She also declared, "There can be no doubt that final victory will be ours."[7]

Let ultimate victory be ours! Aiming for that day, let us advance together harmoniously, resolutely united in the spirit of "many in body, one in mind."

From the August 14, 2003, Seikyo Shimbun

NOTES

1 Translated from Japanese. Leo Tolstoy, *Fumi yomu tsukihi—kotoba wa Kami nari* (Days of Reading—Words Are God), translated by Jirou Kitamikado (Tokyo: Musashino Shobo, 1984), vol. 2, p. 288.

2 Translated from French. Jean de La Fontaine, *Fables contes et nouvelles*, in *Oeuvres complètes* (Complete Works), vol. 1, edited by Jean-Pierre Collinet (Paris: Gallimard, 1991), p. 74.

3 Ibid., p. 154.

4 Ibid., p. 228.

5 Princess Bibesco, *Sir Winston Churchill: Master of Courage*, translated from the French by Vladimir Kean (London: Robert Hale Limited, 1957), p. 9.

6 Translated from Japanese. Soong Ching-ling, *So Keirei senshu* (Selected Writings of Soong Ching-ling), translated from Chinese by Fumiko Niki (Tokyo: Domesu Shuppan, 1979), p. 172.

7 Ibid., p. 173.

The World Is Waiting
for the Victory of Humanism

AUGUST 6, 2003

"The greater the resistance waves meet, the stronger they become."
This has been my motto since I was a youth of nineteen. I have
cited these words innumerable times in my writings.

Surmounting all kinds of obstacles, our movement has steadily
grown, sending forth great waves that are spreading across the
entire globe. Today, the world's leading thinkers and philosophers
are beginning to focus their attention on the philosophy we of the
SGI uphold. This is a development of profound import.

Up to now, here in Japan, the Soka Gakkai has been the object
of every imaginable envious attack because of its commitment to
truth and justice. But intellectuals around the world see things
more clearly, and they express high hopes for the SGI.

The SGI's philosophy of peace is being studied at such leading
universities in the United States as Harvard and Columbia. Publications by the Boston Research Center for the 21st Century, which
I founded, have been adopted by 103 U.S. universities for use in
some 138 courses. In addition, texts used for courses on Buddhism
at many universities also detail the Soka Gakkai's emergence and
subsequent development and its contributions to world peace.

[For example, one such text is Buddhism: Introducing the Buddhist

Experience *by Prof. Donald Mitchell of Purdue University and published by Oxford University Press.]*

Nichiren Daishonin Featured in a New Philosophy Book

The Buddhism of Nichiren Daishonin is also mentioned in *The Big Questions: How Philosophy Can Change Your Life* by Dr. Lou Marinoff, president of the American Philosophical Practitioners Association. Dr. Marinoff believes in the practical application of philosophy to life's problems. One of his earlier books [*Plato, Not Prozac!: Applying Eternal Wisdom to Everyday Problems*] has become a best seller in the United States and has now been published in seventy-five countries.

In *The Big Questions,* Dr. Marinoff said of Nichiren Daishonin:

> Nichiren . . . successfully challenged the corrupt Buddhist religious establishment of his day. Nichiren distilled the Lotus Sutra into a powerful mantra, "Nam-myoho-renge-kyo," which restored the essence of Buddhism to the common people.[1]

[With reference to the emancipating nature of philosophy, Dr. Marinoff also cites a passage from President Ikeda: "Life is filled with truly unfathomable potential. . . . In most cases, our so-called limitations are nothing more than our own decision to limit ourselves."[2] Nichiren Daishonin and President Ikeda are also included in the book's reference list of philosophers.]

Serious interest in Soka humanism is definitely on the rise. In-depth research is being carried out at several renowned universities in China, for example.

[Daisaku Ikeda research groups have been established at around 20

institutions in China, including Beijing University and Anhui University, while Daisaku Ikeda Research Centers have been established at Hunan Normal University, the Guangdong Academy of Social Sciences and the South China Normal University.]

Your earnest daily activities are having a tremendous effect on the world of ideas, helping create a brighter future for all humanity. With pride and conviction in the significance of what you are achieving, please continue your commendable efforts.

Solidarity in a Shared Cause

The world is waiting for the victory of humanism. It is also looking expectantly toward a new era in which women will truly shine. What will enable us to realize those goals?

The Kenyan writer Muthoni Likimani emphasizes the importance of having a sense of unity or solidarity in a shared cause. Recalling the struggle for freedom in Kenya, she reflects that this was the force that enabled ordinary individuals to demonstrate a courage they didn't believe possible.

[President Ikeda was recently presented with a copy of Muthoni Likimani's Passbook Number F. 47927: Women and Mau Mau in Kenya, *a story of her part in the struggle for Kenyan independence.]*

Never Lose Hope!

Never losing hope is also essential. The American author Pearl Buck wrote: "Resignation is something still and dead,"[3] and "Hope is essential for activity."[4] It is important to move forward even just a single step, even just a millimeter.

The French writer Madame de Staël declared to the effect, "We are endowed with a soul or spirit so that we may develop it, perfect it, and use it unstintingly for a higher purpose."[5] We were born in this world so that we could bring forth our fullest potential and shine most brilliantly as human beings.

As the renowned Austrian soprano Jutta Unkart-Seifert, former undersecretary of Austria's Federal Ministry of Education, the Arts and Sport, once observed, "Losing the desire to improve and grow means spiritual death."

Winning Through Wisdom

Many years ago [on April 13, 1957], I had an opportunity to visit the ruins of the mountain fortress of Chihaya [site of one of the most famous battles in Japanese history]. Located near present-day Osaka Prefecture's border with Wakayama and Nara prefectures, the fortress was built by the legendary warrior Kusunoki Masashige.

In 1333, a large enemy force gathered around Kusunoki's Chihaya stronghold. Though he only had a small contingent of warriors under his command, the brilliant general drew on his ingenuity and wisdom. He launched an attack under cover of darkness, using straw dummies to make his force seem larger than it actually was—a tactic that succeeded in throwing his opponents into disarray. Kusunoki's men also dropped boulders over the fort's walls onto the enemy, ultimately driving them into retreat. This masterful defense is recorded in the *Taiheiki*, or "Chronicle of the Great Peace."

Of course, if you have a large force and everything goes according to plan and you have good communications, victory may be relatively easy to attain. But do adverse circumstances preclude victory? By no means. Victory is not determined by externals. What do you do when the odds are against you? Summon forth all the wisdom you can. Wisdom emerges through prayer. Victory emerges through wisdom.

The Soka Gakkai has blazed new trails, bringing hope and inspiration to the forgotten and ignored and making allies of people from all fields and walks of life. That has been the key to our success, to our victorious history.

Allow the Light of Humanity To Shine Forth

As leaders, it is vital first of all that we encourage others with warm, reassuring smiles, constantly striving to impart courage and hope. Leaders mustn't be stuck-up or arrogant or all talk and no action. We must allow our innate humanity to shine forth.

Nichiren Buddhism teaches the concept of the "three bodies of the Buddha" [three kinds of body a Buddha may possess: the Dharma body, the reward body and the manifested body]. Nichiren stated in *The Record of the Orally Transmitted Teachings*, "If in a single moment of life we exhaust the pains and trials of millions of kalpas, then instant after instant there will arise in us the three Buddha bodies with which we are eternally endowed" (OTT, 223). The power of humanity, the light of humanity that shines in your life after you have exerted unimaginable effort in faith—that is the greatest power.

Don't be defeated by yourself. Win over yourself. Return once more to your prime point in faith and challenge yourself anew.

"Worthies and Sages Are Tested by Abuse"

To not be defeated in the face of persecution by arrogant authorities—this is the spirit of faith in Nichiren Buddhism. In a famous passage, he wrote:

When those of rank reproach you for your faith, think of them as worthy adversaries of the Lotus Sutra. Consider it an opportunity as rare as the blossoming of the udumbara plant, or the blind turtle encountering a floating sandalwood log, and reply to them firmly and resolutely. (WND-1, 800–01)

Why are those who uphold faith in the Mystic Law envied? Because they are certain to attain Buddhahood. Nichiren declared:

One who abides by the Lotus Sutra will inevitably attain Buddhahood. Therefore, the devil king of the sixth heaven, the lord of this threefold world, will become intensely jealous of anyone who abides by the sutra. This devil king, we are told, attaches himself like a plague demon to people in a way that cannot be detected by the eye. Thereafter, like persons who gradually become drunk on fine old wine, rulers, fathers and mothers, wives and children gradually become possessed by him and are filled with jealousy toward the votary of the Lotus Sutra. (WND-1, 779)

And it is by overcoming obstacles that we can transform our negative karma and attain Buddhahood. Nichiren also wrote: "Iron, when heated in the flames and pounded, becomes a fine sword. Worthies and sages are tested by abuse" (WND-1, 303); and "If I do not call forth these three enemies of the Lotus Sutra, then I will not be the votary of the Lotus Sutra. Only by making them appear can I be the votary" (WND-1, 53). In perfect accord with these words of the Daishonin, the three presidents of the Soka Gakkai and the organization as a whole have struggled for *kosen-rufu* and made the three powerful enemies appear.

The Path of a Just Life

When someone asked Mr. Toda what made him happiest of all, he replied: "The magnificent development of my disciples who will carry on the struggle for *kosen-rufu*. My greatest joy is meeting and talking with young people." I feel exactly the same way.

The Bulgarian art historian Dr. Axinia D. Djourova said in our dialogue, *The Beauty of a Lion's Heart:* "The person who has a mentor is very fortunate, and the person who can say he or she is someone's disciple is even more blessed. But the greatest joy of all is to have your mentor say that you are his or her disciple."[6] I agree with her completely.

Let me share some of Mr. Toda's comments on leadership with you for the sake of the young people of the future:

> If you only apply yourself to an undertaking with a weak, superficial and perfunctory commitment, how can you expect others to follow you?

> * * *

> Don't be weak-spirited. Be the kind of person who can actualize his or her determinations.

> * * *

> Guidance in faith shouldn't wander off into too much extraneous detail. The point of guidance is to enable people to develop strong faith, so that no matter what difficult challenges they may encounter, they can put the Daishonin's teachings into actual practice and triumph over all hardships. This is true guidance.

* * *

You are not qualified to be a leader unless you genuinely value your fellow members.

* * *

It is vital for youth to have the tenacity to become the very best at something.

Faith equals daily life; and faith manifests itself in society. In this connection, Mr. Toda asserted: "Religion is not some set of abstract concepts; genuine religion is something that is lived, and it must be demonstrated in our lives. Sharing the Daishonin's teachings with others and performing the morning and evening prayers each day are means for improving our lives."

Mr. Toda was an expert on human beings. He offered the following advice for promoting our movement and winning trust in society: "It is important that we make our interactions with others the bedrock of our lives. We are not selling some physical product, we are selling ourselves as individuals." Please talk to others about your faith and convictions sincerely in your own way and with the pride of lofty champions of humanity.

The ancient Greek philosopher Plato declared, "I must dare to speak the truth, especially as truth is my theme."[7] Just speak the truth, exactly as it is. That is more powerful than anything else, and though it may take time, eventually you will get through to others.

Plato also said, "Whoever means to be the right sort of rhetorician must really be just and well-informed of the ways of justice."[8]

We who practice Nichiren Buddhism know the path of a just life, and we are proceeding on the path to a just society. Let us confidently share that truth with others.

From the August 15, 2003, Seikyo Shimbun

Notes

1 Lou Marinoff, *The Big Questions: How Philosophy Can Change Your Life* (New York: Bloomsbury, 2003), p. 343.
2 Ibid., n.p.
3 Pearl S. Buck, *The Child Who Never Grew* (New York: The John Day Company, 1950), p. 57.
4 Ibid., p. 61.
5 Translated from Japanese. Baroness Staël Holstein, *Doitsu ron 3—tetsugaku to shukyo* (Germany, III—Philosophy and Religion), translated by Helene de Groote, et al. (Tokyo: Toeisha, 1996), chap. 12, p. 319.
6 Translated from Japanese. Daisaku Ikeda and Axinia D. Djourova, *Utsukushiki shishi no tamashii* (The Beauty of a Lion's Heart) (Tokyo: Institute of Oriental Philosophy, 1999), p. 263.
7 Plato, *Phaedrus*, in *Plato: Euthyphro, Apology, Crito, Phaedo, Phaedrus*, translated by Harold North Fowler (London: William Heinemann Ltd., 1966), p. 475.
8 Plato, *Gorgias*, in *Plato in Twelve Volumes*, vol. 3, *Lysis, Symposium, Gorgias*, translated by W. R. M. Lamb (London: William Heinemann Ltd., 1967), p. 471.

Treasuring Each Individual
Is the Starting Point of *Kosen-rufu*

NOVEMBER 25, 2003

Who are the most respectworthy of all? It is those who are working for the happiness of others; those who are firmly dedicated to truth and justice. This is a description of our noble Soka members, each and every one of whom is a priceless treasure.

It is imperative that we change the state of the world in which good-hearted, ordinary people are oppressed and forced to suffer. This is an age of democracy, an age where the people are sovereign. Those in even the most powerful positions of authority are there solely to serve the people. It must never be the other way around. Second Soka Gakkai president Josei Toda strictly taught us this point.

It is essential that we treasure and value each individual. This is the starting point of *kosen-rufu*. Let us strive to encourage everyone and warmly embrace and support them. Let us listen to their problems and work together with them for their victory.

Voices ringing with sincerity, voices filled with conviction are an incredible force for good. Words are free, just like the air we breathe. Prayer, too, is free. Though free, they are infinitely important and powerful and form a vital foundation of our lives.

In accord with Nichiren's words "The voice carries out the work of the Buddha" (WND-2, 57), it is crucial that leaders unsparingly use their voices to talk with others. I hope you will sincerely offer words of praise and appreciation to your fellow members, imparting hope and joy to all.

Life Is Action

In my youth, I loved reading the works of the eighteenth-century German poet Novalis [the pseudonym of Baron Friedrich Leopold von Hardenberg]. A pioneer of the Romantic Movement, he proudly declared, "For us, life is action."[1] I was very fond of these words.

As Soka Gakkai members, our greatest pride, too, lies in action. The essence of Nichiren Buddhism is that our actions demonstrate our faith.

The courageous German playwright and poet Bertolt Brecht, who vociferously opposed the Nazis, called out to the people, "It's yourselves you'll be deserting / if you rat on [betray] your own sort."[2]

In a world where human ties are growing ever more fragile and tenuous, what beautiful bonds of trust and friendship exist in the realm of Soka.

This year again, our members across Japan united together with a shared determination to lend every possible assistance to their friends in areas facing daunting challenges. In the spirit of "many in body, one in mind," our entire membership worked hard, persevering tenaciously to the last. That is why we could triumph on all fronts of our movement.

President Toda often used to say even the smallest force could win if it was unified. This is important guidance for us all.

We Have True Friendship

The ancient Greek philosopher Plato said, "The good man is a friend to the good man only; but that the bad man never engages in a true friendship either with a good or a bad man."[3]

There is no room for evil, corrupt people to insinuate themselves into the pure-hearted friendship and unity found in the world of Soka—and that is precisely why such individuals are so envious of us.

As comrades, family, brothers and sisters, fellow human beings, we will fight all our lives for *kosen-rufu*. This is our mission. This is what unites us. We are a fighting force, a fighting fortress.

Allow me to take this opportunity to deeply commend and thank all of you for your tremendous efforts this year. Our repeated triumphs in this Year of Glory and Great Victory [2003] have indeed been significant.

You have accomplished an unprecedented feat—one equal to a decade's achievement. This has been a decisive year in the Soka Gakkai's momentous history. You really made the most amazing efforts and won the most amazing victory! We have never before received such a flood of praise and congratulations from our friends, supporters and leading figures around the world. I am sure all of you have felt this yourselves. From the very bottom of my heart, I would like to applaud and thank all of you for your tremendous efforts. Let's make next year another one of resounding victory!

Accumulating Eternal Benefit Through Our Buddhist Practice

The youth division has grown. This makes me very happy.

The only way we can accumulate lasting and eternal benefit is through our Buddhist practice. Striving earnestly and humbly for the sake of *kosen-rufu*, without airs or pretensions, is what matters. The closing chapters of the lives of those who dedicate themselves in this way will shine with brilliant splendor.

Please become big-hearted people, strong people—indomitable champions of life.

I have engraved in my heart the following words of President Toda, who bravely stood up against Japanese nationalism and remained true to his beliefs even when thrown in jail:

> If you should be imprisoned for championing truth and justice, there's no point losing heart and worrying about when you'll be released. Instead, forge an invincible resolve, telling yourself: "I'm in here for life!"

Mr. Toda was truly a great human being.

Our reaction in one situation highlights the way we will react in all others. Firm determination opens the way forward. Please advance with confidence and strength, armed with the deep conviction that a person who upholds the Mystic Law will never be unhappy and that justice always triumphs in the end.

Corrupt Priests Colluding With the Authorities

In a letter to one of his disciples, Matsuno Rokuro Saemon, Nichiren wrote:

> The fifth volume [of the Lotus Sutra, the "Encouraging Devotion" (13th) chapter] states that after the Buddha's passing, when the Latter Day of the Law arrives, a votary of the Lotus Sutra will certainly appear, and that at that time, in that country, an immeasurably great multitude of monks who either uphold or violate the precepts will

gather and denounce the votary to the ruler of the country, causing him to be banished and ruined. These passages from the sutra all coincide precisely with what has happened to me. I am therefore convinced that I will attain Buddhahood in the future. (WND-1, 892)

In this writing, Nichiren clearly outlined the pattern by which persecution befalls the practitioners of the correct teaching in the Latter Day of the Law, referring to his own struggle based on reading the Lotus Sutra with his life.

In other words, persecution will be caused by corrupt priests, and the means they employ will be defamation and baseless accusations. Furthermore, such priests will collude with unscrupulous individuals who hold secular authority. When practitioners triumph over such onslaughts, their attainment of Buddhahood is certain. This unchanging principle is elucidated in the Lotus Sutra and repeatedly articulated in the Daishonin's writings.

For example, in "The Selection of the Time," the Daishonin wrote:

Such enemies [the powerful enemies of the correct teaching] are to be found not so much among evil rulers and evil ministers, among non-Buddhists and devil kings, or among monks who disobey the precepts. Rather they are those great slanderers of the Law who are to be found among the eminent monks who appear to be upholders of the precepts and men of wisdom. (WND-1, 584)

Further, in "On Omens," he cites a passage from a Buddhist scripture: "Those evil monks will exile and put to death this man of the correct teaching" (WND-1, 647).

In "Response to the Petition from Gyobin," Nichiren wrote:

"The Buddha says in a prediction that the enemies of his teachings will not be evil men like the ones involved in these incidents. He states that it will be monks who resemble arhats with the three insights and six transcendental powers who will destroy his correct teachings" (WND-2, 388).

And in "The Letter of Petition from Yorimoto"—which the Daishonin wrote on behalf of his disciple Shijo Kingo [whose full name was Shijo Nakatsukasa Saburo Saemon-no-jo Yorimoto] to clear him of false charges—he stated: "The Sage Nichiren, the envoy of the Thus Come One Shakyamuni, was exiled because of the false charges leveled against him by the priest Ryokan" (WND-1, 813).

The Hallmarks and Proof of a Votary of the Lotus Sutra

The Soka Gakkai—the noble, harmonious organization that has inherited the Buddha's will and decree—is carrying out *kosen-rufu* in exact accord with Nichiren's teachings. That is precisely why, coinciding with the landmark event of the sixtieth anniversary of our founding [in 1990], we encountered persecution like that predicted in the Lotus Sutra and indicated in Nichiren's writings. We of course have boldly gone on to triumph over that series of obstacles.

Being cursed and spoken ill of, encountering even more hatred and jealousy than during Shakyamuni's lifetime and being attacked by the three powerful enemies are all the hallmarks and proof of a votary of the Lotus Sutra.

["The Teacher of the Law" (10th) chapter of the Lotus Sutra states: "Since hatred and jealousy toward this sutra abound even when the Thus Come One is in the world, how much more will this be so after his passing?" (LS10, 164). The "Encouraging Devotion" (13th) chapter states that the Latter Day of the Law will see the appearance of the three powerful

enemies, including "many ignorant people who will curse and speak ill of us (those who uphold the Lotus Sutra)" (LS13, 193).]

We should be proud that our Soka Gakkai has matched these predictions perfectly.

A votary of the Lotus Sutra is one who fights dauntlessly against great persecution and practices the correct teaching. And a courageous practitioner of the correct teaching is also a courageous seeker of the way.

The Tremendous Growth of Kosen-rufu Is All Due to the Soka Gakkai

As I mentioned at the recent Soka Gakkai Headquarters Leaders Meeting [on Nov. 13, 2003], this month it has been twelve years since the Nichiren Shoshu priesthood sent the Soka Gakkai its Notice of Excommunication [dated Nov. 28, 1991]. We have many new youth now, and for their sake please allow me to once again relate the unfolding of events at that time.

In March 1990, the priesthood, without any discussion with the Soka Gakkai, arbitrarily announced that it was increasing the amounts of monetary offering it would be charging for performing various religious services for lay believers. For example, it raised the offering required for receiving the Gohonzon by 50 percent and doubled the offerings required for inscribing memorial tablets for the deceased [Jpn *toba*] and for conducting perpetual memorial services. This was a highhanded step completely at odds with reasonable standards of decent conduct. In hindsight, it was a clear indication of the priesthood's avaricious nature, which would later be fully exposed.

In April 1990, the No. 2 General Lodging Temple [a lodging for pilgrimage participants] was completed at the head temple under my sponsorship. [The No. 1 General Lodging Temple had been completed in 1988.] In 1990 alone, in addition to this second lodging temple, the Soka Gakkai had built eight branch temples for the priesthood at various locations around Japan. Incidentally, in total, the Soka Gakkai has built 356 temples, 320 of which were built while I was president.

Also, over the years, we conducted countless group pilgrimages to the head temple—the aggregate attendance coming to more than 70 million—and we made concerted efforts to enhance the facilities at Taiseki-ji, including sponsoring the construction of the Grand Main Temple [Sho-Hondo] and the Grand Reception Hall [Daikyakuden].

In the land reforms carried out after World War II, the grounds of Taiseki-ji were drastically reduced to less than 42 acres. Through the Soka Gakkai's contributions over the years, however, the head temple grounds now encompass more than 816 acres, a size unprecedented in the temple's history.

Because of our generous support of the priesthood, successive high priests Nissho, Nichijun and Nittatsu [the 64th high priest, Nissho; the 65th high priest, Nichijun; and the 66th high priest, Nittatsu] expressed deep appreciation and praise for the Soka Gakkai.

In particular, 1990 marked the seven-hundredth anniversary of Taiseki-ji's founding, and to celebrate that occasion, the local Shizuoka youth conducted a wonderful culture festival in September. Yet, while the youth worked so hard on preparations for that event, High Priest Nikken and his cronies were meeting at Taiseki-ji's Tokyo Office in Nishikata, Bunkyo Ward [on July 16], and at a lecture hall on the head temple grounds [on July 18], hatching a plot to destroy the Soka Gakkai, which they called Operation C ["C" standing for "cut"].

This is just the kind of intrigue aimed at obstructing *kosen-rufu* that the Daishonin referred to when he wrote: "People hate me and ceaselessly plot in secret to do me injury" (WND-1, 330). "Evil and unworthy actions such as these on the part of Gyochi continued to pile up day after day..." (WND-2, 826).

During an audience on July 21—just three days after that clandestine meeting at the head temple to plot the Soka Gakkai's downfall—High Priest Nikken lashed out at SGI Deputy President Einosuke Akiya, accusing him of slanderous arrogance. Nikken's loss of composure and his overbearing manner were entirely unbefitting the high priest of a Buddhist school.

The Nichiren Shoshu Priesthood Carried Out a Duplicitous Scheme

Then, in December, as 1990 was rapidly drawing to a close, the priesthood suddenly sent the Soka Gakkai a letter of inquiry. [*This was a document titled "Questions Regarding the Speech of Honorary President Ikeda at the 35th Headquarters Leaders Meeting." This Headquarters Leaders Meeting was held on Nov. 16, 1990, to celebrate the 60th anniversary of the Soka Gakkai.*] It contained a list of the most ridiculous charges—such as the accusation that singing Beethoven's great hymn to universal human freedom, "Ode to Joy," constitutes "praise for non-Buddhist teachings." Furthermore, the priesthood demanded a response to their charges within seven days.

Seeking to find out what had prompted this situation, the top Soka Gakkai leadership made every effort to meet and hold a dialogue with head temple representatives, but the priesthood rejected all such requests out of hand.

Then, on December 27, the priesthood convened a special council session at which they revised the rules of Nichiren Shoshu, thereby dismissing me from the position of head of all Nichiren Shoshu lay organizations and President Akiya and others from the positions of Nichiren Shoshu senior lay representatives. Our members across the nation were stunned by this move. Their New Year's holidays, to which they had been looking forward with such joy and anticipation, were all but ruined. Even now when I think of the pain it caused everyone, my heart aches.

Moreover, in his New Year's message carried in the January 1991 issue of the Soka Gakkai's monthly study journal, the *Daibya-kurenge* [*which went on sale in mid-December 1990 before these events took place*], High Priest Nikken had praised the growth and development of the Soka Gakkai. This was a glaring example of High Priest Nikken being "double-tongued" (WND-1, 324) and "contradicting his own words" (see WND-1, 807), which are regarded as serious offenses in Buddhism. [*High Priest Nikken writes in his 1991 New Year's message in the* Daibyakurenge: *"One of the most notable accomplishments of President Ikeda's leadership, in this postwar period of global human migration and exchange, has been the great advance of worldwide* kosen-rufu *through the establishment of local organizations for the members who have appeared in each country. The steady global development of kosen-rufu we see today is a wonderful event in the history of Buddhism, in accord with the golden words in 'The Selection of the Time.'"*]

At the start of 1991, High Priest Nikken refused to receive Soka Gakkai President Akiya and Soka Gakkai General Director Morita for their customary exchange of New Year's greetings at the head temple, and he shunned meeting with them any time after that as well, stating that they were "unworthy of an audience" with him.

In his writings, the Daishonin described the cowardly manner in which the infamous Ryokan similarly avoided dialogue: "When I actually did return to Kamakura [from exile on Sado], Ryokan shut his gates and forbade anyone to enter. At times, he even feigned illness, saying that he had caught a cold" (WND-1, 482).

High Priest Nikken, like a modern-day Ryokan, behaved in exactly the same fashion.

Nichiren Daishonin Warns of the Nature of False Sages

The Daishonin wrote in detail about the nature of arrogant false sages—the third of the three powerful enemies: "They reveal him [Ryokan] very clearly for what he is. First, though by reputation he is an observer of the precepts, in fact he is wanton in conduct. Second, he is greedy and stingy. Third, he is jealous. Fourth, he holds erroneous views. Fifth, he is lewd and disorderly" (WND-2, 693–94).

The Daishonin clearly exposed Ryokan's true nature. High Priest Nikken is also the epitome of a false sage.

Ryokan persecuted the Daishonin and his followers with every means he could summon. In the same way, High Priest Nikken sought to persecute and cut off the Soka Gakkai.

Allow me to return to the subject of the letter of inquiry sent by the priesthood. Since the priesthood continued to reject our request for dialogue on the matter, we eventually sent a written response in which we protested their unfounded accusations and pointed out the inaccuracies in their transcription of the speech deriving from a tape of questionable origin.

As a result, the priesthood was forced to acknowledge several errors in their transcript, and they retracted the questions related to those fallacious quotations. Their retraction destroyed the entire foundation for their spurious contentions. But instead of issuing an official apology, they then tried to stir up trouble in our SGI organizations overseas and to intimidate and alarm everyone through various means, such as refusing to confer Gohonzon on Soka Gakkai members.

The Banning of Our Members From the Head Temple Is Our Medal of Honor

The Daishonin, referring to the Lotus Sutra teaching that "evil demons will take possession of others," wrote, "He [the devil king of the sixth heaven] possesses…foolish priests such as Ryokan, and causes them to hate me" (WND-1, 310).

Numerous events demonstrate that beneath the plot to disrupt the harmonious unity of the believers lies High Priest Nikken's collusion with what Buddhism terms an evil companion—an individual whom High Priest Nikken himself once denounced as resembling Devadatta [Shakyamuni's archenemy].

The Daishonin wrote, "[In this way] did evil persons throw in their lot with Devadatta" (WND-1, 147), and "Devadatta kept watch on the Buddha's activities and with a large stone caused his [the Buddha's] blood to flow" (WND-1, 146).

In other words, it is as if a modern-day Devadatta and Ryokan joined forces to destroy the Soka Gakkai, an organization faithfully carrying out the Buddha's intent and decree.

The priesthood then sent us a notice announcing that the existing Soka Gakkai-operated monthly pilgrimage system would be abolished. Under a new system to be implemented directly under the priesthood's control, Soka Gakkai members would now have to register with their local temples to obtain the necessary documents permitting them to visit Taiseki-ji. In other words, the priesthood attempted to use pilgrimages as a means to manipulate our members into submission. Their efforts were in vain, however, because our members refused to be taken in or swayed by such tactics.

When the Japanese militarist authorities arrested the first and second Soka Gakkai presidents, Tsunesaburo Makiguchi and Josei Toda, during World War II, the priesthood callously prohibited them and all Soka Gakkai members from visiting Taiseki-ji and any other Nichiren Shoshu branch temple.

Similarly, in 1952, when a group of youth launched their so-called Operation Tanuki Festival, confronting a slanderous priest over his traitorous actions during the war, the Nichiren Shoshu Council convened to dismiss President Toda as Nichiren Shoshu senior lay representative and ban him from visiting the head temple.

President Toda wrote about that latter decision in his "Epigrams" column in the *Seikyo Shimbun* at the time: "I thought I'd receive a reward for my loyalty in rebuking slander of the Law, but instead of praise, they handed me a reproof: 'You're banned from visiting the head temple!' My disciples replied in unison, 'Then we won't visit either, so there!'

"When they asked me, I smiled and said: 'Don't make such a fuss. It's a cause for celebration.'

"As described in the Lotus Sutra, one of the tricks of the three kinds of evildoers is to banish the sutra's votaries 'to a place far removed from towers and temples.'

"Now the Buddha has bestowed upon me the distinguished medal of honor of being banished 'from towers and temples' as proof that I am a great leader of propagation.

"I smiled and asked, 'Are the members of the Nichiren Shoshu Council the second or third of the three powerful enemies?'"

Just as President Toda wisely understood, the banning of Gakkai pilgrimages to the head temple could also indeed be described as a medal of honor from the Daishonin.

The Soka Gakkai conducted and oversaw the running of group

pilgrimages to Taiseki-ji with the greatest care and attention to detail, praying constantly that such visits would take place safely, without accidents. Through these painstaking efforts, we established the brilliant record of welcoming more than 70 million visitors to the head temple [over a 40-year period].

It is quite possible, however, that had our pilgrimages continued at that pace, a major accident may have occurred.

The Daishonin was always deeply concerned about his disciples' safety. With this thought foremost in mind, he urged Shijo Kingo to refrain from visiting him at Minobu as long as the journey there and back remained dangerous.

How immeasurably profound in every sense the Buddha wisdom and the Daishonin's consideration have proven to be.

I am sure that those of you who worked so hard to organize those visits to the head temple and ensure the members' safety will appreciate this ever more deeply as the years go by.

After the excommunication, we received worldwide voices of support.

In November 1991, in what were blatant attempts at intimidation, the priesthood sent the Soka Gakkai an order to disband [dated Nov. 7] and then a notice of excommunication [dated Nov. 28]. Unfazed, however, our members joyfully celebrated the day of our excommunication as signaling our spiritual independence from the corrupt priesthood.

On December 27, a month later—a year after the priesthood dismissed me as head of all Nichiren Shoshu lay organizations—the Soka Gakkai sent a petition demanding High Priest Nikken's resignation from the position of high priest. Some 16.25 million people worldwide signed our petition. So it turns out it was High Priest Nikken instead who had been "excommunicated" by a global alliance of Bodhisattvas of the Earth, 16.25 million strong.

At the same time, upright priests of good conscience took a stand and announced their solidarity with us as comrades in faith dedicated to *kosen-rufu*. All told, thirty temples and fifty-three priests left Nichiren Shoshu. Thoughtful and informed people around the globe also began to speak out in great numbers to support and defend the Soka Gakkai. Today, with gratitude to each of them, allow me to share a few of those statements with you. Professor Nur Yalman of Harvard University is a renowned cultural anthropologist. Following my second Harvard address in September 1993, Professor Yalman told an audience of distinguished educators and scholars that just as the Protestant Reformation had been a landmark event in the history of Christianity, the religious reformation being undertaken by the Soka Gakkai was a development of great significance in the history of Buddhism. The Soka Gakkai's remarkable reform movement, he noted, would have important implications not only for Buddhism but other religious traditions as well. He described it as representing a new departure and a new development in the history of religion.

Dr. David Norton, an eminent professor of philosophy at the University of Delaware, voiced his powerful conviction [in 1991], saying: "The priesthood, in its attack on the activities of the Soka Gakkai, which has been extending a network of peace and culture throughout Japan and the world, is guilty of what can only be described as profound myopia, or even blindness. If asked the cause of that blindness, I'm afraid my only response would be, 'Jealousy.'" He further said, "The priesthood's notice of excommunication goes completely against Nichiren's teaching that all people possess the Buddha nature and that this precious potential must never be closed off or denied."

Great minds outside Japan clearly see the outrageous and foolhardy actions of the priesthood in their true light.

A progressive lay movement stands in contrast to an anachronistic priesthood.

Shin Anzai, professor emeritus of Japan's Sophia University and a leading Japanese sociologist of religion, offered his views as follows: "In recent years the Soka Gakkai has begun to walk a new path as a lay religious organization separate from the priesthood. I view this as an inevitable result of the fundamental difference between the open, progressive Soka Gakkai and the closed, conservative priesthood. The priesthood has become an anachronism, showing no understanding of the value of peace, culture, and education, clinging to hidebound traditions and attempting to control lay followers by authority and force. Had the Soka Gakkai not claimed its independence from the priesthood, it would have eventually been fated to become a self-righteous and closed religious organization, too, its bright future and global development perishing. Japanese intellectuals and journalists need to know this fact, but they completely fail to understand it. I believe this arises from a kind of envy [toward the Soka Gakkai]—the same problem that afflicts the priesthood."

Tetsuro Aramaki, professor emeritus of Kanazawa Seiryo University [formerly Kanazawa University of Economics] and respected economist, observed, "The priesthood, which by rights should be dedicated to the salvation of all living beings, in its demands that the lay body Soka Gakkai disband, shows a callousness totally inappropriate for a religious organization."

In addition, Yukio Kamono of Asahi University, a noted law professor who is also a professor emeritus of Kanazawa University, said: "When I heard about the Notice of Excommunication, in general I must say that I felt it was an arbitrary and extreme measure. To excommunicate an entire organization without any discussion, just a single sheet of paper—from the perspective of normal legal procedure as well—is highly irregular." And Professor Kuniyasu Take of Kyoto's Doshisha Women's College of Liberal Arts argued: "Why is the priesthood seeking to disband an organization of its lay believers [the Soka Gakkai], which is dedicated to the spiritual liberation of people around the world? I feel compelled to point out the suicidal behavior of the priesthood." The courageous statements of these learned figures are certain to shine forever in history.

The Emergence of Lay Leadership Is Inevitable

Dr. Bryan Wilson, reader emeritus of Oxford University and the first president of the International Society for the Sociology of Religion, with whom I engaged in a dialogue published as *Human Values in a Changing World: A Dialogue on the Social Role of Religion*, has written on the matter of our 1991 excommunication: "What emerges from the reactions of the priesthood to this openness to international cultures [of the Soka Gakkai] is the narrow parochialism which prevails within this closed religious caste, cut off from the currents of contemporary thought, and interpreting their spiritual inheritance as a limited and localized experience. . . .

"Without these endeavors by Soka Gakkai, Nichiren Shoshu would have remained an obscure Japanese sect, unknown to the outside world, and perhaps of little significance even within Japan. In affirming Buddhism as a life-affirming religion, Soka Gakkai has rescued Japanese Buddhism from its preoccupations with funeral rites for the dead."

Further, Dr. Wilson shared a positive view of the discontinuation of Soka Gakkai pilgrimages to the head temple, noting that "religious faith transcends all such localized symbolism [as represented by Taiseki-ji]." He continued: "It is by diffusion of commitment and its manifestation in the everyday life and service of believers that a religion develops its influence and fulfills its mission. The particularistic devotion to a place—significant as it may be in the formative period of religious development—must give place to a universalistic spirit if that religion is to become a major influence in world affairs."

Dr. Wilson also called the emergence of lay leadership in religion as part of an inevitable historical process, and his assertion has now been borne out beyond a doubt.

To Betray the SGI Is To Betray Nichiren Daishonin

I have also published a dialogue with the French art historian and champion of the human spirit, René Huyghe, titled *Dawn After Dark*. Mr. Huyghe remarked that the world should thank the Soka Gakkai for promoting the profound values and universality of Buddhism, as well as for its efforts to advance world peace by elevating the human spirit based on Buddhist ideals. Anyone, he said, would surely lament disreputable attacks motivated by hunger for power or material gain that might hinder the Soka Gakkai's admirable efforts to uplift humanity and its splendid success.

Dr. Howard Hunter, now emeritus professor of religion at Tufts University in the United States, said [in 1991] that he was very interested in observing what kind of effect the excommunication of more than 10 million lay followers by a tiny minority of priests claiming orthodoxy would have on the priests themselves, since it was such an extraordinary thing to do. He added that when a religious group loses touch with the hearts of its followers who are striving earnestly to apply their religious beliefs in society and the real world, that group is on the road to ossification.

Twelve years have passed since we received the Notice of Excommunication from the priesthood. As all of you are well aware, our victory in light of Buddhism is crystal clear.

The Daishonin recorded the fate of Ryokan and his colleagues: "You may think that those who believe in Priest Two Fires [Ryokan] are prospering, [but this is certainly not the case]" (WND-1, 638). The strict retribution befalling High Priest Nikken and his cohorts is proof that they have been excommunicated and condemned by the Daishonin himself.

Today, all of the aberrations of Nichiren Shoshu have been laid bare for the world to see: the plot to try to destroy the movement for *kosen-rufu*, the false creed of worshiping the high priest, the erroneous view of the true heritage of Law, the misuse of priestly ceremonies and services, the discrimination that places priests above the laity and the general corruption and degeneration that pervade the school.

In contrast, the Soka Gakkai has become the pillar of Japan and a bright light of hope for the world. It celebrates its seventy-third anniversary this year with a global network that spans 186 nations and territories [now 192] and with an unprecedented tide of victories.

The Daishonin, the Buddha of the Latter Day of the Law, undoubtedly praises us and smiles on our efforts, while at the same time commanding the protective forces of the universe to keep us safe from harm.

I am equally sure our victory would bring immense delight to President Makiguchi. Our founding president once observed: "How much more serious is the offense of those Buddhist and Shinto priests who stand even further upstream and put poison into the water. In this case, even a small transgression can become an extremely grave offense, making a cause that will bring infinitely evil retribution. How much graver still it is then to oppose great good and contribute to great evil, to bow to great evil and slander great good."

I have always fully agreed with these words. In fact, it is the great evil of High Priest Nikken and his cohorts that resents and envies the great good of the Soka Gakkai.

As champions of the correct teaching, we have resolutely triumphed over the schemes of such malicious forces.

President Makiguchi also said: "The more others slander and despise the Lotus Sutra, the greater the happiness [its votaries will ultimately come to experience as a result of this persecution]. We are certain to win in our struggle. The important thing is to put the principle of 'changing poison into medicine' into practice in our lives."

On another occasion, he said, "The harder we fight and the stronger we become, the more swiftly actual proof of victory in our Buddhist practice appears." We have fought in exact accord with the words of the Soka Gakkai's founder. That is why we have been victorious.

"The final fate of all traitors is a degrading story of suffering and ignominy," said President Makiguchi with keen perception. What he says is absolutely true, as you have seen with your own eyes.

President Toda also declared: "To betray the Soka Gakkai is to betray the Daishonin. You'll know what I mean when you see the retribution they incur at the end of their lives."

And in discussing the Daishonin's "Letter from Sado," he said: "The Daishonin declares that when evil priests ally themselves with evil rulers and persecute those who seek to establish the correct teaching, those who fight against such iniquity with lion-hearted courage will surely attain Buddhahood."

President Toda further said: "The Soka Gakkai spirit is to work for the happiness of our country and all countries in the world. . . .

The purpose of *kosen-rufu* is to make it possible for all the world's peoples to live in happiness." And he declared: "Let us be as proud as lion kings! For, according to *The Writings of Nichiren Daishonin*, that is how we will become Buddhas—'as Nichiren did.'"

The Daishonin admonished strictly: "Both teacher and followers will surely fall into the hell of incessant suffering if they see enemies of the Lotus Sutra but disregard them and fail to reproach them" (WND-1, 747); "Rather than offering up ten thousand prayers for remedy, it would be better simply to outlaw this one evil" (WND-1, 15); and "From now on too, no matter what may happen, you must not slacken in the least. You must raise your voice all the more and admonish [those who slander]" (WND-2, 597).

These are all passages that President Makiguchi and President Toda frequently referred to and cited.

Let us also never relax in our struggle, fighting on for justice to the very end, just as the Daishonin teaches.

Salute to a Warrior of the Pen

Today, November 25, is the hundredth birthday[4] of the Chinese writer Ba Jin, with whom I have met and spoken on four occasions. I sent the renowned author a congratulatory telegram on this magnificent milestone. Praying for his continued long life, I would like to share with you some of the words of this venerable warrior of the pen who also fought against persecution.

Steadfast in his belief that truth and justice would prevail, he wrote:

> When I say that evil can never triumph over good, I am saying that in every society there is a struggle between right and wrong, between light and darkness, and the final victory must always belong to justice and light.[5]

He has also said: "Just as a castle built on sand will never be indestructible, power built on lies will never endure,"[6] and, "You cannot lie to yourself."[7]

Ba Jin has always held out hope that the people would become strong and wise, saying, "The people are the best judge."[8] He further stated:

> One thing is certain: If the majority of the people possessed a solid, self-reliant philosophy or independence of mind, refused to be blindly subservient, and spoke out for and had faith in the truth, the ugliness and hypocrisy of the world would be much diminished.[9]

Ba Jin firmly believes in the importance of standing up for what is right:

> The fates of many people have strengthened my own firm and unwavering conviction. That conviction is that the purpose of life is in giving, in being of service, not in receiving or in acquisition.[10]

And:

> If you make a start, others will advance behind you. If you take the first step, the second will be easier. If someone takes the lead, he will not be lacking in others to follow after him. In this way, the number of people walking this path is sure to increase.[11]

I pray for the continued vigorous endeavors of all of you, my precious fellow members, who are leading the way on the path to world peace and happiness for all humanity.

Faith Is the Driving Force for Victory

In closing, I would like to share with you some words that I have been fond of since my youth.

The first are from the American poet Walt Whitman, who sang in his *Leaves of Grass*, "I would be the boldest / and truest being of the universe."[12] Be the boldest, truest beings in the universe! Let's make that our goal.

The ancient Greek dramatist Sophocles wrote, "In any question the truth has always greatest strength."[13] There is no weapon stronger than the truth.

An Ch'angho, a leading architect of Korean independence who is often described as Korea's Gandhi, declared, "Be determined to accomplish ten things in the time others accomplish one." Determination is the key to growth and the source of strength.

A famous passage from the Buddhist scriptures [which is cited by Nichiren] states:

> If you want to understand the causes that existed in the past, look at the results as they are manifested in the present. And if you want to understand what results will be manifested in the future, look at the causes that exist in the present. (WND-1, 279)

By taking up a determined struggle in the present, we will create a victorious future filled with hope and happiness. Ultimately, by triumphing now we ensure our future triumph.

Faith is the driving force for victory. I therefore call on all of you to charge ahead vibrantly, living out your lives with lionhearted courage.

Looking toward the Year of Total Victory of Soka [2004], I am praying that you will enjoy the best of health and advance dynamically, filled with hope.

As we bring this meeting to a close, let's make a determination and a promise to one another to take the first powerful step toward great victory.

From the November 28 and 29, 2003, Seikyo Shimbun

NOTES

1 Translated from German. Novalis (Friedrich von Hardenberg), "Alle Menschen Seh Ich Leben," in *Gedichte und prosa* (Poems and Prose), compiled by Herbert Uerlings (Dusseldorf and Zurich: Artemis & Winkler Verlag, 2001), p. 119.

2 Bertolt Brecht, *Bertolt Brecht: Poems 1913–1956* (London: Methuen Drama, 1984), p. 185.

3 Plato and Xenophon, *Socratic Discourses* (London: J. M. Dent and Sons, Ltd., 1954), p. 216.

4 Ba Jin actually turned 99 this year [2003], as he was born on Nov. 25, 1904, but it is the tradition for Chinese to celebrate their living relatives' centennial birthday at the age of 99. (According to China's *People's Daily,* Nov. 25, 2003.)

5 Translated from Japanese. Ba Jin, *Mudai-shu* (A Collection of Untitled Essays), translated by Takashi Ishigami (Tokyo: Chikuma Shobo, 1988), p. 78.

6 Translated from Japanese. Ba Jin, *Shinwa-shu* (A Collection of True Stories), translated by Takashi Ishigami (Tokyo: Chikuma Shobo, 1984), p. 157.

7 Ba Jin, *Mudai-shu*, p. 95.

8 Translated from Japanese. Ba Jin, *Zuiso-roku* (Essays), translated by Takashi Ishigami (Tokyo: Chikuma Shobo, 1982), p. 15.

9 Translated from Chinese. From an article written by Ba Jin's daughter, Li Xiaolin. <http://www.chinanews.com.cn/n/2003-11-21/26/371822.html> (Nov. 21, 2003).

10 Translated from Japanese. Ba Jin, *Byochu-shu* (While Battling Illness), translated by Takashi Ishigami (Tokyo: Chikuma Shobo, 1985), p. 112.

11 Ba Jin, *Mudai-shu*, p. 53.

12 Walt Whitman, *Leaves of Grass* (New York: Dutton, 1968), p. 392.

13 Sophocles, *Fragments,* edited and translated by Hugh Lloyd-Jones (Cambridge, MA: Harvard University Press, 1996), p. 413. Fragment 955.

Index (Volumes 1 and 2)

Archias, Aulus Licinius 1: 80;
Cicero's defense of 1: 81
Aramaki, Tetsuro, priesthood's
attack on the Soka Gakkai,
comment on 1: 130
Arendt, Hannah 2: 23
Aristotle 2: 5, 8, 44, 67
arrogance 1: 67 2: 5; form of 1: 19;
guarding against 2: 57; Josei
Toda on 2: 12, 25; and leaders
2: 56
Asahi University 1: 130
Ashoka, on gratitude 2: 105
attitude, arrogant 1: 2; benefits
of maintaining pure 1: 10;
inner 2: 39, 76; negative
2: 56; Nichiren Daishonin
highlighting importance of
2: 76
authority, position of 2: 87;
secular 1: 50
Aylwin, Patricio 2: 105

Ba Jin, quotes of truth and justice
by 1: 135–36
backslide, never 2: 39
Bagabandi, Natsagiin, Daisaku
Ikeda, appreciating 2: 109
beauty, true 1: 10
behind the scenes, recognizing
people working 2: 83
Beijing University 1: 107, 2: 55
beliefs, Nichiren Daishonin
describing people of
steadfast 1: 98; steadfast
1: 74
belittle, Josei Toda describing
reason not to 2: 83

benefits, basis for gaining
immense 2: 112; scope of 2: 26
Bergson, Henri-Louis 1: 11
Bharat Soka Gakkai [SGI-India]
1: 44
Bibesco, Marthe 1: 102
*The Big Question: How Philosophy
Can Change Your Life*
(Marinoff), Daisaku Ikeda
quoted in 1: 106; study of
Nichiren Daishonin in 1: 106
birth rate, positive view of the
decline in 2: 40
Bodhisattva of the Earth,
Nichiren Daishonin outlines
the spirit of 2: 69
Boston Research Center 1: 3, 105;
impact of the works published
by 2: 52
brand-new, spirit of always
starting 1: 86
Brecht, Bertolt 1: 116
Buck, Pearl 1: 107
Buddhahood, attaining 1: 110, 2:
64; path of attaining 2: 26
Buddhas 2: 24; becoming 1: 99;
behavior of 1: 19; Josei Toda
outlining way to become
1:134–35; Nichiren Daishonin
outlining criteria for attaining
2: 108; noble work of 2: 31;
obstacles to attaining 2: 95;
will of 1: 120
Buddhism 2: 97; battle in 2:
13; cause for destroying
2: 96; consequence of not
admonishing the enemies
of 2: 62; essence of, 36;

fundamental spirit of 2: 88; life of 1: 38; Nichiren Daishonin defining outcome of practicing 1: 88; Nichiren Daishonin stating lifeblood of 1: 50; Nichiren Daishonin's warning about internal enemies of 2: 95; number eight in 2: 37; power of 1: 7; practicing 1: 8; principle of 1: 31, 60; purpose of 2: 12–13; struggle in 2: 103; teaching of 1: 13, 38, 60, 2: 22, 45, 115; true 2: 33; way of 2: 51

Buddhism: Introducing the Buddhist Experience (Mitchell) 1: 105

Buddhist, model of a true 2: 24

Buddhist compassion, Josei Toda describes 2: 25

Buddhist members, effect of meeting 1: 18; respecting 1: 12

Buddhist Order, action against individuals disrupting the unity of 2: 118–19; action against precept-violating priests in early, 2: 119; instances of corrupt practitioners in early 2: 118–19

Burnett, Frances Hodgson 2: 82

Caribbean, and SGI members 2: 26

caring, Josei Toda's emphasis on 2: 15

Carson, Rachel 1: 86

cause and effect, Buddhist law of 1: 12, 2: 25, 91

censure, Tsunesaburo Makiguchi on 1: 62

Chang-an 2: 91

Ch'angho 1:137

challenge 1: 109; Buddhist handling 2: 107

champ, true 2: 107

character, 2: 83; cultivating outstanding 1: 31, 2: 94; developing 1: 37; education and 1: 13

Chartier, Emile. See Alain

cheerful 2: 107

Chihaya (mountain fortress) 1: 108

children, and encouragement 2: 121; and kindness 2: 121; lasting memories in 2: 121; qualities needed for raising 2: 121; raising 1: 62

Chuko K'ung-ming 1: 54, 56, 65, 2: 38; Daisaku Ikeda's impression of philosophy of leadership of 1: 68; evaluating character, methods of 1: 72–73; stating attributes of superior leader 1: 69

Churchill, Winston 1: 102

Cicero, Marcus Tullius 1: 77–78, 83; and Buddhism 1: 51; European culture, influence on 1: 77–78; evil and corruption, weapon against 1: 79; on friendship 1: 80

Columbia University 2: 52

commitment 2: 108

community, basis for transforming 2: 112;

mentor-disciple relationship, Daisaku Ikeda's reason to advance the path of 2: 3–4; Josei Toda outlining 2: 17, 72; Nichiren Daishonin outlining 2: 2; significance of studying spirit of 2; 108; spirit 1: 14, 33–34 2: 7, 73–74; true Soka spirit of 2: 11; to youth division 2: 16

mentors 2: 2

Milton, John 1: 31; on ingratitude 2: 67

mind, frame of 1: 11; inspiring peace of 2: 83; Nichiren Daishonin expounding power of 1: 35

mind-set 1: 46; overcoming fixed 1: 96

misery, basis of human 1: 44

misfortune, path to 1: 60

mission 1: 37, 95–96; benefits of realizing one's 1: 74; carrying out one's 2: 46; place of 1: 14; unique 2: 108

Mitchell, Donald 1: 105

momentum 2: 106

Mongolia, Nichiren Daishonin lamenting execution of the envoys of 2: 109–10; Soka Gakkai representatives visit to 2: 109

Mongolia-Japan relations, Soka Gakkai's contribution toward 2: 109–10

Mongolian University of Arts and Culture 2: 109

Morita, Kazuya, Nikken's behavior toward 1: 124

mothers 1: 28

motivation, inspiring 2: 84

Mount Minobu 1: 23

Mukherjee, Bharati 2: 2

Mystic Law 1: 60, 2: 51; benefit of practicing 1: 118; life dedicated to 2: 2; Nichiren Daishonin expounding benefit of propagating 1: 100; Nichiren Daishonin stating benefit of propagating 2: 86; Nichiren Daishonin's instructions to rely on 1: 43; power of 1: 11, 2: 45, 108; securing path for prosperity of 2: 22–23; scope of 1: 95

Nagarjuna, on gratitude 2: 105

Nagashima, Danny 2: 51; achievements under leadership of 2: 79–81

Nanjo Tokimitsu 1: 92

Nam-myoho-renge-kyo 2: 48; chanting of 2: 49; Josei Toda stating benefit of chanting 1: 23. *See also* Mystic Law

National Language Bureau, of SGI-USA 2: 80

nationalism 1: 5

nations, causes for failure of 1: 81–82; criteria for growth and prosperity of 1: 45; foundation for building trust among 1: 93; prosperity of 1: 67; treasure of 2: 43; Tsunesaburo Makiguchi highlighting factor threatening the future of 1: 36

Nationwide Executive

behavior of, matches
Shakyamuni's describing
one type of ascetic 2: 110–11;
cause for the spiritual decay
of 2: 38; greedy nature of
1: 121; and Josei Toda, 127;
path of 1: 88; peculiarity of
1: 133 "Questions Regarding
the Speech of Honorary
President Ikeda at the 35th
Headquarters Leaders
Meeting" 1: 123; scheme of 1:
122–26; and *shakubuku* 2: 30;
Soka Gakkai's contribution to
1: 122; Soka Gakkai's petition
and 1:128; and Tsunesaburo
Makiguchi 1: 127
Nichiren, writings of 2: 61, 67;
Josei Toda's emphasis on
reading 2: 17; reading 2: 17–18
Nightingale, Florence 1: 46
Nikken 1: 88, 122, 125–26; and
behavior 1: 122; being "double
tongued," example of, 122–24;
"contradicting his own
words" example of 1: 122–24;
Daisaku Ikeda's leadership,
praising 1: 124; praising Soka
Gakkai 1: 124; retribution
1:133
Nikko Shonin 1: 23
Nissho, and Soka Gakkai 1:122
Nittatsu, and Soka Gakkai 1: 122
Nomonhan, Battle of 2: 110
Norton, David, priesthood's
attack on the Soka Gakkai,
views of 1: 129; the
priesthood's Notice of

Excommunication, comments
about 1: 129
Novalis 1: 116
Nkrumah, Kwame 1: 61

obstacles, benefit of overcoming
1: 110; encountering 1: 101
"obstacles equal peace and
comfort," in practice 1: 60
Oceania, *kosen-rufu* movement
in 2: 41
oneness of mentor and disciple
1: 28
Operation C, aim of 1: 122.
See also Nichiren Shoshu
priesthood
Operation Tanuki Festival 1: 127
opinions, leaders and 2: 51
opponents, Nichiren Daishonin's
unyielding conviction against
1: 100; Nichiren Daishonin's
view of 1: 99–100
opportunities, seizing 1: 66
optimistic 2: 107
organizations 1: 21; basis for
growth of 2: 19–20,104; cause
for stagnation of 2: 20; cause
for the decline of 2: 56; causes
for failure of 1: 81–82; criteria
for growth and prosperity of
1: 45; decline of, 2: 38; factors
to advance growth of 2: 31;
growth of 1: 67; Josei Toda
stating reason for protecting
1: 20; mark of humanistic
1: 46; and reform 2: 20;
requirements for successful
1: 71; spirit for growth of 2:

Russia 1; 89; and SGI members
2: 26
Ryokan, modern-day 1: 126
(*See also* Nikken); Nichiren
Daishonin describing
cowardly manner of 1: 124–25;
Nichiren Daishonin outlining
true nature of 1: 125; Nichiren
Daishonin records fate of
1:133

Sado Island 1: 97
Saito, Kenji 2: 112
Sakurai, Hiro appointed as
committee president of
Religious Nongovernmental
Organizations 2: 81
Sammi-bo, Buddhist practice
2: 120; Nichiren Daishonin
records the fate of 2: 120
Schiller, Friedrich von 2: 6, 93
Schopenhauer, Arthur, on envy
1: 31
seeking spirit 2: 89
Seikyo Shimbun 1: 2, 53; aim of
2: 31; Josei Toda affirming
mission of 1: 52
self-improvement, key to
2: 3; limitless 1: 31, 2: 72;
Tsunesaburo Makiguchi on
1: 31
senior members, source of pride
for 2: 39
sense of responsibility,
manifesting 1: 91
SGI, goal of 1: 20–21; growth of
1: 105; implications of growth
of 1: 37; and Josei Toda 1: 21;

mission of 1: 9; reason for
development of 2: 107–08;
significance of betraying 1:132;
spirit of, 28; 30th anniversary
of 1: 97; world leaders and
1: 31
SGI activities, benefit of carrying
out 2: 4
SGI-Italy 1: 82
SGI members, mission of 2: 45;
strength of 2: 48
SGI movement 1: 2
SGI organizations, causes
for decline of 1: 19; and
Nichiren Shoshu priesthood's
intimidations 1: 125–26
SGI Plaza 2: 80
SGI-South Korea (KSGI),
development of 2: 41
SGI-USA, Culture of Peace
for the Children of the
World exhibition of 2: 80;
development of 2: 41; growth
and development of 2: 79–81;
resource centers of 2: 80–81
SGI-USA New York Culture
Center 2: 80
Shakespeare, William 2: 57
shakubuku 1: 31; emphasis on
practicing 1: 23; Josei Toda
expounding benefits of
practicing 1: 23; leaders and
2: 29; Nichiren Daishonin and
2: 29; Nichiren Daishonin
expounding effects of
practicing 1: 22; purpose of 2:
29; spirit of 1: 83
Shakyamuni Buddha, final

Ikeda and 2: 98; Daisaku
Ikeda's impression of 2: 98
training, benefit of strict, 2: 94;
youth division members and
2: 94
traitors 1: 51; Josei Toda's
warning against, within Soka
Gakkai 2: 25; Tsunesaburo
Makiguchi describing fate of
1:134
"true mission" 1: 29
trust 2: 67; building 1: 18;
creating mutual , between
senior and junior members 2:
5; Daisaku Ikeda's remarks
about 1: 52; foundation for
building 1: 93; Josei Toda on
1: 53; Josei Toda's advice for
gaining, in society 1: 112; way
for leaders to win people's
2: 102
truth 1: 44; benefit of speaking
out for 2: 72; conveying 1:
90; defeating 2: 45; gaining 2:
117; labeling people against
defending 1: 80; path to
unending triumph of 2: 3;
power of 2: 56; speaking out
for 1: 112, 2: 47; weapon of
1:137; words of 2: 68
Ts'ao Ts'ao 1: 65
Tsedev, Dojoogiin 2: 109
Tufts University 1:132
twentieth century, human life in
1: 3
twenty-first century, 3; hopes for,
97; human society in 1: 3
2010, Soka Gakkai in 2: 37

understanding, way for leaders
to gain people's 2: 102
unfocused, effect of being 1: 61;
Josei Toda's strictness toward
2: 115
universities, and capable
people 2: 120; study of SGI's
philosophy in, 105–06
University of Bologna 1: 82, 2: 67
University of Denver 2: 106
University of Massachusetts 1: 2
unity 1: 1, 71, 2: 18, 48; basis
for true 1: 44; building 1: 55;
creating mutual, between
senior and junior members
2: 5; guarding against
individuals destroying 2: 117;
Josei Toda and 1: 116; need
for 2: 6; Nichiren Daishonin
describing importance of
maintaining 2: 96; Nichiren
Daishonin outlining benefit
of 1: 61
Unkart-Seifert, Jutta 1: 108
Ushio (magazine) 2: 21, 104

value, key to achieving new 1: 59
value creation, life of 2: 33
victors, 1: 46, 85–86; Nichiren
Daishonin describing 1: 7
victory 1: 28, 102, 2: 106; Buddhist
formula for 1: 61; cause for
1: 7; cause for daily 2: 115;
creating cause for next 2: 56;
determining, under adverse
conditions 1: 108–09; driving
force for 1: 137; formula for 2:
51; Josei Toda stating cause for

praising 1: 57, 88; earning the trust of, by youth division 1: 43; efforts of 2: 4, 43, 86–87; hopes for 1: 46; Josei Toda cheering activities of 1: 56–57; Josei Toda encouraging 1: 56; and leaders response time 2: 5; male leaders and 2: 38; men's attitude to 2: 4–5; praising 2: 87; respecting 1: 13, 28 2: 86; "radiance" of 1: 87; role of 1: 59; spirit of 2: 76–77; and white lilies 2: 43; youth division and 1: 12

women's division leaders, appreciating 2: 22; priority of 2: 89

words 1: 115

words and letters, Nichiren Daishonin stating importance of using, for *kosen-rufu* 2: 31

work, consequences for leaders avoiding hard 2: 102–03

works, Daisaku Ikeda reasoning for sharing words of great 2: 89

world, reason being born in 1: 108

world peace 1: 83; eternal path to 1: 102. *See also kosen-rufu*

World Tribune, growth of 2: 80

World War II, 2: 48; Japanese economy and society after 2: 12

Yalman, Nur, and Soka Gakkai reform movement 1: 129

Yamatai [ancient Japanese kingdom] 1: 5

Year of Glory and Great Victory (2003), Daisaku Ikeda expressing gratitude to members in 1: 117

years, determining factor in the final 2: 32

Yokota, Masao 2: 52

young men's division leaders, and challenges 2: 85; spirit of 2: 86

youth, call to 2: 116; challenge apt for 2: 84; developing 1: 12; hopes for 2: 8, 76; Josei Toda's call to 2: 44; path of 2: 44; period of 1: 91; power of 2: 16; power of energy of 2: 116; quality for 2: 72; raising 2: 72; role of 1: 12; spirit of, 21; training of 2: 33, 121; treasure of 1: 52

youth division, challenge for 1: 30; Daisaku Ikeda's commitment to 1: 53; efforts of 2: 4; encouragement to 1: 117–18; greatest life for 2: 36; growth of 2: 32; hallmark of 2: 102; hopes for 1: 34, 2: 16, 37–38, 83, 91, 113; and injustice 1: 36; Josei Toda and 2: 32; Josei Toda declaring spirit of 1: 29, 33–34; Josei Toda stating basis for attaining true greatness to 2: 12; Josei Toda encouraging 2: 16; Josei Toda's hopes for 1: 22; and *kosen-rufu* 1: 33; mission of 2: 37; and propagation 2: 32; silence and, 11; and Soka Gakkai meetings

More Reading on Nichiren Buddhism

FROM MIDDLEWAY PRESS

These titles can be purchased from your local or online bookseller, or go to the Middleway Press Web site (www.middlewaypress.com):

The Living Buddha: An Interpretive Biography
BY DAISAKU IKEDA
The first in the three-volume Soka Gakkai History of Buddhism series
An intimate portrayal of one of history's most important and obscure figures, the Buddha, The Living Buddha chronicle reveals him not as a mystic but as a warm and engaged human being who was very much the product of his turbulent times. This is a biography with a double focus. It is a vivid historial narrative based on what is known or can reasonably be surmised concerning the Buddha's life and time. It is also an inspiring account of a heroic life dedicated to helping all people free themselves from suffering and futility and attain true peace of mind.
(Middleway Press, paperback: ISBN 978-0-9779245-2-3; $14.95)

Buddhism, The First Millennium
BY DAISAKU IKEDA
The second in the three-volume Soka Gakkai History of Buddhism series

A major effort to formulate the Buddhist canon took place not long after the death of Shakyamuni Buddha at what is known as the First Council. Subsequently there arose differences of interpretation and a schism between the monastic community and the lay community. Nevertheless, Buddhism survived and developed. It came into contact with the West and spread eventually into Southeast Asia, China, Korea, and Japan. Contributing to this process were certain individuals—exceptional rulers like the Indian king Ashoka and the Greek philosopher-king Menander, in addition to monks and lay believers, including Vimalakirti, Nagarjuna, and Vasubandhu. Buddhism, The First Millennium portrays the coming of age of what is today a major world religion.
(Middleway Press, paperback: ISBN 978-0-9779245-3-0; $14.95)

FROM WORLD TRIBUNE PRESS

These titles can be purchased at SGI-USA bookstores nationwide or through the mail order center (call 800-626-1313 or e-mail mailorder@sgi-usa.org):

Kaneko's Story: A Conversation with Kaneko Ikeda
Kaneko Ikeda shares thoughts and stories of her youth, marriage and family and of supporting her husband of more than fifty-five years, SGI President Daisaku Ikeda. Also included are four messages written to the women of the SGI-USA.
(World Tribune Press, mail order #234302; $9.95)

My Dear Friends in America
By DAISAKU IKEDA
This volume brings together for the first time all of the SGI president's speeches to U.S. members in the 1990s.
(World Tribune Press, paperback: SKU #204891; $15.95)

The New Human Revolution
By Daisaku Ikeda
An ongoing novelized history of the Soka Gakkai, which contains episodes from the past as well as guidance in faith that we can apply today.
(World Tribune Press; $12.00 each volume)

Volume 1, mail order #4601
Volume 2, mail order #4602
Volume 3, mail order #4603
Volume 4, mail order #4604
Volume 5, mail order #4605
Volume 6, mail order #4606
Volume 7, mail order #4607
Volume 8, mail order #4608
Volume 9, mail order #4609
Volume 10, mail order #4610
Volume 11, mail order #4611
Volume 12, mail order #4612
Volume 13, mail order #4613
Volume 14, mail order #4614
Volume 15, mail order #275446
Volume 16, SKU #275447
Volume 17, SKU #275448